The International Library of Sociology

INDUSTRIAL INJURIES INSURANCE

Founded by KARL MANNHEIM

<u>*The International Library of Sociology*</u>

THE SOCIOLOGY OF WORK AND ORGANIZATION
In 18 Volumes

I	Apprenticeship	*Liepmann*
II	Industrial Disputes	*Eldridge*
III	Industrial Injuries Insurance	*Young*
IV	The Journey to Work	*Liepmann*
V	The Lorry Driver	*Hollowell*
VI	Military Organization and Society	*Andrzejewski*
VII	Mobility in the Labour Market	*Jeffreys*
VIII	Organisation and Bureaucracy	*Mouzelis*
IX	Planned Organizational Change	*Jones*
X	Private Corporations and their Control (Part One)	*Levy*
XI	Private Corporations and their Control (Part Two)	*Levy*
XII	The Qualifying Associations	*Millerson*
XIII	Recruitment to Skilled Trades	*Williams*
XIV	Retail Trade Associations	*Levy*
	(The above title is not available through Routledge in North America)	
XV	The Shops of Britain	*Levy*
XVI	Technological Growth and Social Change	*Hetzler*
XVII	Work and Leisure	*Anderson*
XVIII	Workers, Unions and the State	*Wootton*

INDUSTRIAL INJURIES INSURANCE

An Examination of British Policy

by

A. F. YOUNG

ROUTLEDGE
Taylor & Francis Group

First published in 1964 by
Routledge

Reprinted 1998, 2000, 2002
by Routledge
2 Park Square, Milton Park, Abingdon, Oxon, OX14 4RN

Transferred to Digital Printing 2007

Routledge is an imprint of the Taylor & Francis Group

British Library Cataloguing in Publication Data
A CIP catalogue record for this book
is available from the British Library

Industrial Injuries Insurance
ISBN 0-415-17677-8
The Sociology of Work and Organization: 18 Volumes
ISBN 0-415-17829-0
The International Library of Sociology: 274 Volumes
ISBN 0-415-17838-X

Publisher's Note

The publisher has gone to great lengths to ensure the quality of this reprint but points out that some imperfections in the original may be apparent

CONTENTS

Contents

THE ISSUES

ACKNOWLEDGEMENTS

MANY have helped in the development of this work, and to them all I want to express my sincere gratitude; especially to Mr. G. H. F. Mumford and Mr. K. C. Clarke, Clerks to the Southampton Magistrates, and to Mrs. P. Dunn, Mrs. J. Grubb, Mrs. I. Bason and Mrs. P. Powell for their tolerance and patience in typing the script; and to Miss D. Marshallsay and Miss O. Simpson for their help in the index and in proof-reading.

INTRODUCTION

THIS is a study of policy; of why and how the United Kingdom has developed financial provisions for workers injured in the course of their employment. It is an inquiry not so far undertaken in Britain since Sir Arnold Wilson and Professor Levy published their monumental book on *Workmen's Compensation* in 1939. It was the passion and erudition of their writing that provided the impetus for this further investigation to see what changes, if any, had occurred since the abolition of the old workmen's compensation law, and the initiation of the new industrial injuries legislation.

In launching such a study it was necessary to impose certain limitations. For instance, a mass of legal and administrative items was available in the laws that were passed and the regulations that were promulgated. If the general principles of policy were not to be buried under a load of detail, it was necessary to confine the analysis to those matters affecting the trends of policy alone. Major modifications, such as the decision to extend disablement benefit to the very earliest stages of pneumoconiosis, were added to the text, but to include a survey of the vast array of regulations and Commissioners' decisions seemed pointless. Nor was an examination of the position in the coal mines undertaken, not because it was unimportant, nor tragically productive of accident and disease, but because its inclusion did not appear materially to alter the principles involved, nor the general picture of the provision for injured workers. As for the material used to illustrate the study, it was as recent as the exigencies of publication allowed. The time span since 1948, when the industrial injuries contributory scheme began, has been long enough to demonstrate the general trends, and complete enough to provide adequate information within a reasonable perspective. Unless and until a fundamental change is brought to the whole scheme, the weaknesses and strengths of the policy will in all probability remain much as they have emerged in the present investigation.

Though the provision of cash benefit for the injured worker is the core of the study, there were other important factors to consider. Insurance benefit is paid because men and women suffer accidents and diseases in the course of their employment, and some indication of the extent of occupational illness in those industries covered in Britain by the Factory Acts became a vital part of the evidence. Thus Part I is concerned with factory accidents and diseases, and the voluntary and statutory efforts to mitigate the dangers and promote safety.

Part III, on the other hand, deals with a very different aspect of industrial injury, but one that is intimately associated with the future of the injured man, with his insurance benefit, and with his employer. An appreciation of the ancient right to seek 'alternative remedies' could not be omitted from a work of this nature, and accordingly an attempt has been made to elucidate the problem, not so much from the legal angle, but from the viewpoint of social policy. In doing so, the case of employers, criminally liable for defection in their statutory duties, has received comment but no analysis, since the book was not primarily concerned with them. Criminal liability is an important problem, and further inquiry into the whole conception of punitive action against the negligent demands urgent attention.

If there are conclusions to be drawn from this scrutiny of the industrial injuries scheme the most fundamental would be to question the wisdom of prolonging so lugubrious, and in some ways so unjust, a means of benefiting injured workers. This is not to argue in favour of the immediate abolition of the scheme, without suitable alternatives, but to suggest that what was relevant in the late nineteenth century is not necessarily so in the last half of the twentieth. The hazards of modern society which make injury to its citizens a common phenomenon, and the complexities of the scheme itself lead inexorably to the conclusion that preferential benefit for those injured or diseased 'arising out of and in the course of employment' is no longer justified. Less fundamental, but interesting and paradoxical, is the striking similarity in detail between the workmen's compensation and the industrial injuries' schemes. For of changes there have been few. But what there were have been made in the most telling quarters, and for this reason the whole spirit of the service has been revolutionized.

PART ONE

Industrial Accidents and Diseases

THE rise of the factory system brought this country much social change and great wealth, but it also increased the amount of maiming and the loss of life among its operatives. Concern over the high accident rate was early expressed in a series of government reports and private memoranda, written to attract public attention to what was obviously a serious and growing social evil. In a sense these documents have made encouraging reading to observers in the late twentieth century, since they have shown from what gross neglect and danger our forefathers rescued us. At the same time the number and nature of twentieth-century industrial accidents have given no grounds for complacency; and the widespread concern, from the government to the smallest factory, has been an indication that a total of nearly 200,000 accidents per year in factories alone is not tolerated without strenuous efforts being made to reduce them.

Before a closer analysis of the figures of British experience can be made it is necessary to examine some of the bases upon which they were compiled. The figures published annually by the chief inspector of factories have related solely to industrial undertakings which came within the meaning of the Factory Acts, excluding offices and shops,* farms, mines and quarries, and premises where no machinery was used. They covered only a percentage of all employed persons and related to a more restricted field than those of the Industrial Injuries Act, to which reference will be made in Part II. Any comparison of the two sets of figures is accordingly impossible. Even within the field covered by the Factory Acts, reportable accidents were limited to those involving death or loss of time for over three days, cuts and bruises not resulting in the loss of time being excluded. As for any international comparisons, the pitfalls were manifold. To industrialized countries like Britain the usefulness of the word

* To be included after 1963, as a result of the Offices, Shops and Railway Premises Act, 1963.

'industrial' was appropriate, but in countries where agriculture dominated the economy, the term was not. The word 'accident' might have several meanings. A catastrophe like an accident in a mine involving many people might be listed as one accident, while in other cases the number of persons affected would be the basis of enumeration. Nor was the word 'injury' satisfactory, as a person might suffer multiple injuries through a single accident, and in certain countries the term was even used to cover diseases, as in the British industrial injuries legislation. Some countries based their statistics on the happenings that resulted in compensation, but this had its drawbacks as the systems of compensation varied so much. Statistics useful for comparative purposes were consequently very hard to come by, and all that could be said was that there was an international concept to be studied 'based on the number of persons involved (killed or disabled) in industrial or work accidents, or through industrial or occupational diseases'.[1] As early as 1923, at the first international conference of labour statisticians convened by the International Labour Office in Geneva, member states agreed to collect statistics on industrial accidents, and classify them according to industry, cause, degree of disability and the location and nature of the injury. They agreed also to use the device of frequency and severity rates to calculate comparative numbers of accidents and the time lost through them, but while figures collected by each country were explicable within the context of that country, international comparisons were still precarious, and in any case the undertakings were not always implemented.

Bearing in mind this caution, it appears that some of the older industrialized countries were on the whole more successful with their safety measures than the newer. It was a lamentable fact that when a country was developing its industry, it seemed to learn so little from the gruesome past history of those who were first in the field. Two examples would serve to illustrate this: there was the contrast between the United Kingdom and the United States on the one hand who in the 1950's had only about half the number of fatal accidents proportionate to their working population as Japan; and there was the case of India, whose industrial accidents increased alarmingly during the same period. Of course India and Japan were developing countries with abundant manpower where rapid industrialization was the aim and where, though compensation for industrial accidents was available, safety precautions were not so highly developed.

Turning now to the industrial accident position of Britain itself, it is the aim of Part I to assess the trends since 1948 in crude numbers, in the distribution by industry, age, sex and geography, to see what influence is exercised by the size of the factory, to tackle the thorny problems of cause and remedy, and thus to analyse the social setting in which the industrial injuries benefit scheme operates.

I

AN EXAMINATION OF BRITISH FACTORY ACCIDENTS

Numbers

THE numbers of work accidents have tended to fluctuate and those in 1962 (190,158), although an increase on 1958 (167,697), compared reasonably with 1948 when 201,086 persons were injured, but not so favourably with 1938 (180,103). Thus after over twenty years of the most intensive efforts to make industry safety-conscious the results were hardly encouraging. On the other hand, during the war years accidents increased greatly owing to war conditions, and the numbers in employment during and after the war were much larger, making the post-war difficulties considerable, both in offsetting the poorer safety traditions of the war years, and in ensuring that accidents did not rise with the numbers employed.

A more refined indication of trends would have been the use of the 'frequency rate'* where the number of accidents is related to 100,000 man-hours worked (roughly the number of working hours in a lifetime), but this method had its limitations as the information was supplied voluntarily and therefore intermittently by interested firms. The accident frequency rate in 1962 was 1·66 or nearly seventeen per million man-hours worked; no accurate comparisons with the situation in 1948 were possible since the firms responding to the request for figures were not the same.

* The Frequency Rate is calculated as follows:

$$\frac{\text{No. of accidents causing absence from work}}{\text{Total man-hours worked}} \times 100{,}000$$

Industrial distribution

Accidents varied in seriousness from industry to industry, but apart from a comparison of fatal with total accidents there was no satisfactory way of estimating industrial distribution.* In one of the best years (1957) the overall ratio was one death to every 270 non-fatal accidents, but the spread was uneven, for whereas in building and in metal extracting there was one death for every ninety other accidents, at the other end of the scale, in textiles, there was only one death in every 930 accidents. During the period fatal accidents in docks, warehouses, building operations and constructional work tended to decline, though the total number of accidents in these industries did not. If compared with 1938, when the deaths were 944, experience after the war was perhaps more satisfactory.† On the other hand, the margin between life and death in a serious accident is very narrow and dependent to a large extent on the quality and availability of medical services. Mindful of the modern advances in medical science, in the use of drugs, in the availability of ambulances and hospitals, and in the industrial medical services, the overall reduction in deaths was smaller than might have been expected.

Fatalities are only one measure of an industry's vulnerability, frequency is another. In so far as 'frequency rates' have any reliability, it would appear that apart from coal mining, the most dangerous of all industries, the frequency rates in 1962 indicated that coke ovens (4.37) bacon curing (3.03) and brewing (3.45) were some of the centres where accidents were most common. The relative position of the various industries (apart from mining) tended to fluctuate from year to year, but on the whole it was the metal manufacturing, engineering and constructional trades which showed a higher incidence of accidents than others.

Building, particularly, had been a source of concern for years. In 1951 it was described as the most dangerous industry, largely because it tended to be impermanent, without the same care being exercised in erecting safety devices, keeping rights of way clear, seeing that scaffolding and ladders were safely erected. In fact the chief inspector of factories has more than once declared that half

* The sixth international conference of labour statisticians held in Montreal in 1947 recommended the calculation of a 'severity rate', but no regular calculations of this kind were made in Great Britain.

† The total of fatalities fluctuated, and was 668 in 1962.

the accidents in building could have been prevented if more care had been taken to supervise, provide protective clothing, maintain a proper standard of housekeeping, and above all to train the workers in safety methods. In such an industry high standards of physical fitness were always necessary, because the jobs involved climbing and working at a height, often on strenuous work. Good eyesight was essential to a worker who might otherwise walk into a hole or slip, but care in maintaining these standards has not been adequately exercised. Figures for this industry have fluctuated through the years, as they have in others. By 1957 it seemed that the corner had been turned when a 16 per cent fall in accidents was announced. The very next year showed not only an overall rise in the number of accidents, but an increase in deaths.*

Accidents at Building Operations

	Total	*Fatal*
1952	12,702	207
1956	14,820	186
1957	14,568	156
1958	15,017	207
1961	18,742	174
1962	19,986	193

Age distribution

How far the number of accidents increased because the worker was young or old was naturally of importance in considering the total problem of industrial injuries, and an aspect to which the chief inspector of factories gave much thought in his reports.

(a) Old Age

The employment of the elderly attracted attention because conditions of full employment made it necessary to use all available

* Mr. P. J. Thomas, the then Parliamentary Secretary to the Ministry of Labour estimated that the cost of accidents to the building industry was about £20 millions a year, the equivalent of seven shillings a week for every worker engaged in the industry (*The Times*, 4.2.60.). Lord Taylor, industrial medical officer in Harlow, estimated the total cost of ill-health and accidents in industry as a whole as being of the order of £780 to £1,000 millions a year. (Speech in House of Lords, 28 April, 1959.) In America W. D. Keeper, in an article on 'Accident Cost' in *Industrial Safety*, 1953, ed. R. P. Blake, estimated the annual costs of industrial injuries as about £600 per person injured.

labour, and because population changes, involving an increase in the proportion of the elderly to the total population, directed public attention to them as a social problem, and also because the modern popularity of superannuation and other pension schemes increased the number retiring in their sixties. Several inquiries have therefore been made into the suitability of the elderly to continue in work, and the Ministry of Labour itself set up a national advisory committee on the employment of older men and women (with local advisory committee counterparts) whose objects were twofold: to inquire into the problem, and to persuade employers to find suitable jobs for the elderly.

On the specific aspect of accidents among older workers evidence was conflicting. It was shown that accidents occurred because a person was elderly, with slower reactions, less supple muscles, more brittle bones, and perhaps deficient hearing or sight. For instance a young man and an elderly man were sitting on a form waiting for a solution of caustic soda in a tank to be heated by means of a steam coil. Suddenly there was an escape of steam and the solution spilled over. The young man jumped on to the form and escaped injury. The older man tried to get to the door, slipped on the floor and was fatally injured by the spillage of the caustic soda.[2] Moreover, age would not necessarily involve greater carefulness, and it would be useless to think that a person who had taken risks all his life would reform when older. For example a man of sixty wanted to cross a pit in a railway workshop. Ten feet away was a permanent gangway but, because this meant a detour, he elected to walk across a temporary platform nineteen inches wide which happened to be handy. He slipped and fell into the pit.[3] Falls were a major cause of accident among the elderly, perhaps because they had foot and leg trouble which made them less stable on their feet. For instance a man of sixty-seven fell in a factory yard as he was hurrying to catch a bus and was badly injured. The factory inspector, who reported this, also added that this same man had already worked from 7.30 a.m. to 7 p.m.![4]

In spite of the foregoing, the general evidence did not support the common assumption that older workers necessarily sustained more accidents, proportionately to the young. On the contrary, statistics supplied to the national advisory council by the Ministry of National Insurance in 1953 showed that the rate of award of injury benefit was nearly twice as high among men under thirty as over sixty, and though the older person required longer sick leave after an accident than the younger one, the average number of days lost by those over sixty was only slightly higher than that for all age groups together. One of the main reasons why the older worker had fewer accidents than the young was that he was less subjected to risk. There was a tendency for him to leave the more hazardous occupations before he became too old, and management frequently employed him on a less dangerous job, even though the firm as a whole was engaged in dangerous operations. On the other hand where experience was a factor in avoiding accidents, the older man had usually learned to take care of himself, and was therefore at an advantage.

The chief causes of accidents to the older workers were from the handling of goods, from falls, or being hit by falling bodies, or themselves striking against objects. But as these ranked highest in the causes of all accidents, irrespective of age, there was little significance in the figures.

The Ministry of National Insurance figures quoted above suggested that the older worker tended to have longer sick leave after an accident than younger people. It would be hard to say whether this was because the accidents were more severe, or because an accident took more out of an older person, or because the relatives, and perhaps the doctor, tried to encourage him to absent himself longer in order to be fully recovered before returning. Some have thought that an accident could often be the touch point for retirement, either because the man himself lost heart, or because the relatives decided the moment had come. It would seem that if the elderly were to continue in employment, early return to work, even if it were to a light job, was to be encouraged.

But the provision of special employment for the elderly was very uneven. Some firms made separate arrangements for them such as shorter hours or early knocking-off time to avoid peak travelling hours; or they provided work on less dangerous machinery. There was no general arrangement, and the provision of 'light work' for the elderly, as indeed for any worker whose work potential had been reduced by accident or other causes, had little meaning, unless it were a job a man was able to do at his own firm or a similar one, and one reasonably near his residence.

Jobs of this sort were not readily available, and were too rare to accommodate all for whom they were recommended.

Fatalities among older workers occurred, but not significantly more than among younger people. The fatality rate among those over sixty was 0·075 per 1,000, and 0·055 per 1,000 among those under sixty.[5] Nor did the industrial distribution of accidents provide evidence that any one industry was specially dangerous to the elderly as such. The total number of accidents to old people reportable under the Factories Acts was 13,192 in 1961, compared with a total of 192,517 for all workers in the same year or about 7 per cent; this represented a slightly lower proportion than that of elderly to all workers in industry (8·7).

(*b*) *The Young*

Industrial accidents to the young were a problem of 'green' labour, and the number remained obstinately high (12,423 in 1962 and 13 killed) in spite of legislation, safety propaganda, training and all the other methods that have been used with increasing persistence through the years.

Under Sect. 21 of the Factories Act, 1937, strengthened by a number of special regulations, it was an offence for an occupier to fail to train and supervise a young person in the use of 'dangerous machinery', a list of which was supplied by successive Orders-in-Council. Thus a young person was prohibited from working on certain machines unless he had been fully instructed on the dangers inherent in them and the precautions that had to be observed. Further, until he had received sufficient training he worked the machine only if under the supervision of a person with a thorough knowledge and experience of it.

Employers themselves showed much interest in their young workers and tried in most cases to comply with the statutory requirements, both because they were statutory, and because they wanted the youngsters to be safe and happy working for the firm. Even so since 1948, of all reportable accidents throughout industry, 7·5 per cent was the average annual contribution of young people. Of these, boys suffered more than twice as many as girls. The annual reports of the chief factory inspector recorded increasing concern about this situation and on several occasions he expressed himself forcibly: 'Allowing young persons to be injured or killed is a form of extravagance in which British industry simply cannot afford to indulge. . . . Young persons constitute industry's most precious raw material, and employers would do well to ask themselves if they are watching over it with all the care that it needs.'[6]

Many instances were available of how some, albeit a small minority, of employers carried out their statutory duties of training and supervision. A seventeen-year-old girl received severe lacerations to three fingers of her left hand when her hand slipped on to the cutters of a knife-handle-shaping machine, which she had been in the act of stopping. Not only were the electrical gear of the machine and the guard for the cutters defective, but investigation showed she had received only half an hour's tuition on the machine from the charge-hand, who was a deaf-mute.[7] This happened in 1952. Mutilation of the hands by woodworking machinery was all too common, and showed a wilful disregard of the woodworking machinery regulations. On the other hand the best of training and oversight by the foreman could not prevent every accident, as the anticipation of some would need almost super-human prescience. For instance, the raggy cardigan sleeve of a boy of fifteen caught between the end of a stripper roller and the cylinder in a woollen mill and his hand was crushed.[8] A girl, also of fifteen, had her head caught under a descending platform because she enjoyed the experience of watching it come down.[9] It would be hard to foresee accidents of this sort.

It has been thought by qualified observers (the factory inspectors) that the ratio of accidents due to machines was higher among young persons than adults, and that the greatest single cause was lack of proper instruction. As the chief inspector has said: 'Instruction is frequently left either to an adult who is incapable of properly instructing, or who is thoughtless, or, worst of all, who sets a bad example by his own conduct. Not infrequently the instruction is left to another young person barely older than the newcomer. Even if the instruction is given by a suitable person, it is often much too perfunctory, not through any lack of goodwill, but through a simple failure to grasp the reiteration and practice that is needed, before the average young person is really taught. It should be added that the amount of patient instruction required to teach the not-so-bright, and to make sure that they have really learned what they have been taught, is quite incredible to those not experienced in such persons.'[10] It has been suggested that very dangerous machines, like cutting presses in the boot and shoe trade, should not be used by youngsters, unless they have had adequate experience on less dangerous machines first.

Many firms had great difficulty in finding suitable people to act as foremen and supervisors. Yet they were crucial to proper training and safeguarding. Also, many trainers seemed to forget how they had felt when they first started work, and appeared not to appreciate the adjustment a boy or girl had to make on leaving school and first going into a factory. On the other hand discipline was not always easy to enforce under conditions of full employment and labour scarcity.

The young themselves should not be absolved from blame. Some of them were so eager to make more money that they took risks. A boy of sixteen was put on a power press, fitted with an interlock guard, on a Saturday morning. The charge-hand showed him how to make three or four components, and then left him to proceed on his own. On the following Monday the boy asked if he could remove the guard so that he could work faster. The charge-hand removed the guard for him and on the Tuesday one of the lad's fingers was crushed between the tool and the die.[11] The charge-hand was clearly to blame for removing the guard, and for not giving effective supervision, but the boy himself, as in many other similar cases, had been anxious to earn higher wages, even though the higher output meant dispensing with the guard. There have been instances of a juvenile causing an accident by trying to be helpful. For example a boy of fifteen was killed in a carpet loom. The weaver was absent and the boy went into the loom to clean it, though he had not been told to do so. When the weaver returned, he set the machinery going, not knowing the boy was inside.[12]

Young people have often been blamed for 'skylarking' and there have been instances of accidents arising out of play. It has been known for boys or girls to climb on to a roof (to retrieve a ball, or to have their lunch) too flimsy to bear their weight. This kind of accident could have been prevented if adequate foresight had been exercised by the management, or proper warnings given. Even so the general impression was that 'skylarking' was not a major cause of industrial injury. Curiosity was the cause of a few accidents. There was one laconic account of a young boy of fifteen who had his hand scalded when he 'put it into a barrel of water to see if it was hot. It was!'[13]

What was least understandable was where a firm disregarded the advice of the appointed factory doctor. Thus in 1953 a boy was certified as unfit to work on a machine because of defective eyesight. Yet in spite of this he was actually employed as a 'taker-off' on a partially unfenced rotary board-cutting machine. In grabbing a piece of broken cardboard, his hand touched the tool and he lost the top of his right forefinger.[14]

Whatever the cause of the accident, the young were accident-prone because they were new and inexperienced. A substantial number of accidents happened within a few days of their starting work. Dr. Lloyd Davies, at that time chief medical officer to Boots Pure Drug Company, stated in 1948 that 15 per cent of young people under sixteen had accidents.[15] In America some years ago (1924) the Bureau of Labour estimated that 81 per cent of the accidents in the steel trade happened on the first day of employment, when a large number of new entrants were the young. However, it was agreed that without training, supervision and constant vigilance, accidents would go on. People did not suddenly change at eighteen or twenty-one, and the responsibility of the older worker for the young was very great, whether he were his supervisor or not. For the young copied the older workers – their faults as well as their virtues.

Sex differences

Accidents to men and boys have always been higher than for women and girls, mainly because the jobs they have done have been intrinsically more dangerous, and perhaps too because women and girls were less venturesome and less inclined to take risks. On the other hand women were also, on the whole, less machine-minded and might expose themselves to risks through ignorance. The number of accidents to males was about six times as great as for females (e.g. 1962 = 155,000 males, 23,000 females). This could be partly explained by the disproportion of male to female employees (about $2\frac{1}{2}:1$) but there were clearly other factors. The industrial safety committee estimated in 1956 that, since the war, the average proportion of accidents to males per 1,000 employed had been about thirty, while to females it was about ten.[16]

The proportion of ten per 1,000 for women and girls was regarded as somewhat high by the factory inspectors, especially as the rate remained substantially unchanged for a number of years. It was suggested that the number of injuries could be reduced if more attention were paid to the problem. The adult woman re-entering employment after a break due to family responsibilities was frequently 'green' labour, just as much as the youngster fresh from school. It might be asked whether the same care in training and safety precautions was given to her as to the young? Further, because girls and women were usually employed on safer jobs, extra care was sometimes not thought so necessary for them. The chief factory inspector in 1954 commented that, where firms gave special attention to accident prevention, accident frequency rates among females showed a decline.

Geographical distribution

It would be hard to make any sustained comparison between the accident rate in various parts of the country, as the basis upon which the published figures were calculated was altered in 1952, and again in 1958. However, as might be expected, areas of heavy industry, like the north and Scotland, had more accidents than other places, while centres of light and new industry such as London and the south-east, had fewer. What was disturbing was that the north and Scotland showed no decline in their figures, in fact between 1952–6 there was a marked increase which had still not been halted by 1961. The same was true of London and the south-east, though in these cases the figures remained steady, rather than increasing. The parts of the country where accidents were shown to be declining were in the south-west, Wales and the Midlands.

Experience in separate industries differed somewhat from the overall picture provided year by year in the factory inspectors' reports. Thus, the chief safety officer of the Electricity Council has given us a glimpse of the situation in that industry (generating mainly) for the last quarter of 1958.[17] The frequency rate showed the south-east as highest (3·22), while the north-east (1·92) and the north-west (1·69) were relatively low. On the other hand the duration rate* was highest in the southern area (316), lowest in the south-east (144) and Midlands (160), fairly low in the north-west (187) and fairly high in the north-east (281). He also calculated the severity rate.† This showed the Midlands again having a good record (292), while South Wales soared up to the top of the scale (722). The south-east came midway (464).

Size of Factory

Another aspect of the industrial injuries problem was the size of the working unit itself. One tends to think of the small factory, with its lack of capital resulting in few safety devices, as being potentially a more dangerous place to work than the large well-equipped concern able to invest in all the latest safety precautions. Such a view would be misleading. For in fact the number of accidents tended to rise proportionately with the size of the factory. The chief factory inspector, reviewing the situation in 1954, found that in a factory with ten or fewer employees the average number of accidents per year was at the rate of ten per 1,000 employees, and the rise in the rate was steady until, in those factories employing more than 2,000 workers, the accidents per year were at the rate of over twenty-eight per 1,000 workers. Thus the larger the factory the more accident-prone it appeared to be. This did not imply that the larger factory was less safety-conscious; on the contrary, it might be more so than its smaller brethren. The explanation was partly in the type of work done. Accidents were more prevalent in heavy than in light industry, and as small-sized factories tended to be concerned with light industry, their accident potential was smaller. When a survey of similar-sized engineering factories was made in 1954, it was found that those undertaking heavy engineering had an accident rate of thirty-eight per 1,000 employees, in medium engineering it was eighteen, and in light engineering it was only thirteen. The nature of work done in the large factory might be one explanation but not the whole one. The reason why factories, on the average, tended to be safer when

* Duration Rate $= \dfrac{\text{Number of man-hours lost}}{\text{Number of accidents}} \times 100{,}000$

† Severity Rate $= \dfrac{\text{Number of man-hours lost}}{\text{Number of man-hours worked}} \times 100{,}000$

they were small merits considerably more thought and research than has yet been given.

The Site of the Injury

One would expect an accident to the head or trunk to be more serious clinically than one to any other part of the body; but accidents to the limbs, especially the hands or feet, may be just as serious to the man's chances of continuing in his employment, or obtaining a job of similar status and pay. The figures produced by the factory inspectors on the siting of the injury showed remarkable similarity of pattern year by year. More than one in three accidents were to the arms, shoulders, hands and fingers (39 per cent), and rather fewer to legs, ankles, feet and toes (31 per cent). Only 18 per cent were to the trunk, and 6 per cent to head and neck. The limbs were therefore the most vulnerable parts of the body, and it was a serious matter that about seven out of ten injuries were to these members. In 1961 a closer examination was made and it was found that in accidents connected with machinery (other than lifting) three out of four injuries were to the hands and arms. In accidents involving transport about one in three injuries were to the feet.

Accidents to the eyes, though very serious when they occurred, accounted for only about 3 per cent of all injuries, or between 6,000 and 7,000 a year. This however was not a true picture of eye vulnerability, as most eye accidents, being minor ones, were not reported. If they were, it is estimated the number would be more like 200,000 a year. In 1950 an analysis of eye injuries by industry and age was made. It was found that two in three were in the metal manufacturing, engineering and allied trades, and that fitters and machine erectors were the chief sufferers, with foundry workers next, and metal machinists in third place. Only about one in forty were in the building industry, but of these about half were to building labourers. Men had about twenty times more eye injuries than women, which could easily be explained by the differences in their jobs.

The analysis made no mention of the relative numbers employed in each age group and this clearly affected the figures. But in the table supplied by the chief factory inspector of 1950, more than half the eye injuries were shown to have occurred to men between twenty and forty years. Youngsters did not show such a serious proportion, and, when over forty, the numbers tailed off until they reached insignificant proportions between sixty and sixty-five. After that age there was a rise, but the number of eye injuries to those over sixty was under one in eight in 1950, which might have been the result of greater experience, or because the jobs became less hazardous. It is difficult however to understand why the numbers remained so high up to forty years, as a man would reach a considerable degree of skill and experience long before that.

Timing of Accidents

Some indication of days and months dangerous to the eyes was also given. Wednesdays and Fridays were the worst, with Saturdays and Sundays the best. As for the months of the year, the worst were in the winter from September to March (except December) though, counting absences on holiday such as Christmas, Easter and the two summer holiday months of July and August, the months did not vary very much. It was also found that eye accidents rose steadily during the morning until dinnertime, fell again in the early afternoon and rose again between 4 p.m. and 5 p.m. It was thought that the reason for this was, that at the beginning of the day the work was preparatory in character, but later the pace increased and the liability to accidents rose. This did not explain why Wednesday and Friday should differ from the rest of the week. Whether the pattern was similar for accidents as a whole in this country we do not know. But in 1950 a survey was made by Zetterman of the experience in Sweden.[18] He found the peak accident period per day was between 9 a.m. and 11 a.m., and between 2 p.m. and 3 p.m. As both peak periods coincided with the latter end of a shift (6 a.m. to 4 p.m. being the common work span in Sweden) fatigue has been put forward as an explanation. It may, on the other hand, have been a time when concentration began to slacken, as the end of the work span approached. Whatever the reason, the overall experience in Sweden was not dissimilar from that revealed by the limited survey of accidents to the eyes made in this country and, were the timing of accidents studied more closely, more light might be thrown on the complex issue of cause, the subject of the following section.

Causes of Accidents

Much has been thought and written on this aspect of the problem, and year by year the factory inspectorate have collected statistics on the industry and process where the accident happened, the age and sex of the injured persons, the immediate cause of the accident, and the parts of the body that have been affected.

In coding the information so obtained some arbitrary decisions have had to be taken. For instance, in deciding upon the 'cause' of an accident, there was usually more than one event that could reasonably be selected and a choice had to be made. As a rule what seemed the most important event was chosen. In practice, the choice fell on the event involving the contravention of a legal requirement, or the event where action should have been taken to avoid the accident or, in cases of multiple injury, the event which led to the most serious injury. In situations of this kind any classification under a single heading would be liable to misrepresentation, and the information contained in the tables must therefore be read with considerable caution.

The Human Factor

In Britain the 'human factor' in accidents has not been included as one of the causes, perhaps because it was *ipso facto* present in all accidents, but in many countries much has been made of it, and it has been common when considering causes to distinguish two groups: those due to technological, mechanical or physical causes, and those due to unsafe behaviour by the worker. The relative importance of these groups has been expressed in the proportion of 15:85.[19] On the other hand it has been seldom that an accident was due wholly to the one or the other, but rather to an amalgamation of a group of circumstances, only one of which would be unsafe behaviour.

The American Standards Association[20] have evolved a scheme, which, if it were generally adopted, would obviate altogether the necessity of stipulating the cause. This scheme has analysed the accident under five headings:

(1) The agency, and agency part concerned, e.g. the machine, the hoist, the boiler.
(2) The unsafe mechanical or physical condition encountered, e.g. improperly guarded, poor illumination, unsafe dress, passages not kept clear.
(3) The type of accident, e.g. striking against the object, being struck by it, a fall, being caught in a machine, contact with dangerous fluids.
(4) The unsafe act committed, e.g. taking away the guard, working without authority, operating at unsafe speed.
(5) The unsafe personal factor involved, e.g. lack of knowledge or skill, bodily defects, disobedience.

The following is an illustration of the method:[21]

A fifteen-year-old boy had the job of cleaning the gangways of a workroom and was told not to clean under the machines. When he saw oil on the floor under a rope-making machine, he cleaned that part of the floor also and, as he did so, the cotton waste used for cleaning became caught between two gear-wheels just above the floor; these were protected by a hood on the top and sides but not at the bottom. As he tried to pull out the cotton, his hand was caught between the gears and badly mutilated.

The analysis of this accident according to the American recommended practice would be:

(1) (*a*) Agency	= Machine (Rope-maker)
(*b*) Agency part	= Gears
(2) Unsafe mechanical or physical condition	= Inadequately guarded
(3) Accident type	= Caught between gears
(4) Unsafe act	= Operating without authority
(5) Unsafe factor	= Wilful disregard of instructions

This accident was clearly due to the presence of a variety of factors, any of which alone would not have resulted in an accident. Thus, if it had been the human factor alone and the boy had, contrary to instructions, cleaned underneath a machine where the gears were not exposed, his hand would have remained undamaged. Or, so long as everyone obeyed instructions the unguarded gears were safe. But because a disobedient boy came in contact with gears that ought to have been fenced, an accident occurred.

Because the 'incident' or 'near accident' could be as much a pointer to the presence of danger as a serious accident itself, many undertakings have required that 'near accidents' should be reported and the situation investigated as carefully as a serious one would be. Such firms calculated that for every occurrence causing serious injury, twenty caused minor ones and two hundred no injury at all. But, in their view, investigation of the two hundred was as important as of the one. In the light of such considerations the formal British statistics of industrial accidents were a mere pointer to the danger lurking in the industrial situation, and the misleading nature of the items that stated the cause (or apportioned the blame) became apparent.* Since these statistics were the only ones available, we had to learn what we could about the causes of accidents and the reasons for them from such information as there was.

The evidence indicated that in spite of the increasing use of power-driven machinery, and the presence of numberless lethal objects in the factory and workshop, most accidents did not arise from these but were, in the main, due to ordinary causes like handling goods, using hand-tools, or by the operative himself falling, or being struck by a falling object. In fact, only one in six accidents in factories in the period was due to power-driven machinery, while in other workplaces like ships, wharves, building sites and engineering construction sites the proportion was even smaller, being one in eleven. Nor was Britain alone in this. For in 1958 more than one in three of the accidents in France were due to the handling of goods, while machines accounted for just over 10 per cent. In New Zealand machines were a bigger danger (20 per cent), but in the U.S.A. a limited statistical survey of deaths through industrial accidents in six States showed that about one in ten was caused by machinery.[22]

Of all causes of accidents in this country those under the heading 'the handling of goods' remained, as in France, persistently at the top. Nearly one in three of all accidents in factories was due to this cause. It is not immediately apparent why this should be. Obviously goods have to be moved about in a modern

* From 1947 certain 'dangerous occurrences', such as the failure of a crane, have been compulsorily reported to the factory inspector, whether they resulted in accidents or not. But as they have covered only a tiny proportion of the total 'dangerous occurrences' (1,533 in 1962), they are to be discounted.

factory to an increasing extent, and the means of transport themselves constitute a danger. There has been a growing tendency towards 'palletization,' i.e. the stacking of materials on pallets as unit loads and carrying them on fork-lift trucks. Some firms have gone so far as to issue booklets on the safe driving of these trucks, including such advice as: Carry the load in front unless it obstructs vision; clear the path rather than go round objects; keep the load near the floor and allow no one to ride on it except to control the load, etc.[23] But in spite of this, accidents continued to happen. Not that the use of motorized transport was the chief bugbear; hand-trolleys and even the manual carrying of goods often led to disaster. While handling of goods was a necessary concomitant of industry, it was clear that the human factor was a large part of the situation, though how to draw the line between the human element and the 'perversity of the inanimate' was not easy.

Another group of accidents, where the human element was clearly uppermost, was where the occurrence could be classified as 'persons falling, stepping on, or striking against objects, being struck by falling body'. The latter has been included in this group, because the 'falling body' was so often dropped by other workers, as on building sites, or was due to the victim not keeping a sharp look-out. The group accounted for another third of the accidents in factories. Even the use of hand-tools was responsible for a respectable proportion of accidents – about one in twelve. Thus the machines used for manufacturing, and the molten metal necessary for some processes, which might have been thought the greatest source of danger in modern industry, accounted for only a fifth of all accidents in 1962, a proportion that has remained fairly steady in the post-war years. The guards, fences and other safety precautions, now statutory duties on all employers, have apparently curbed what might have been a growing menace to life and limb. No effective explanation has been given of why accidents through 'falling' remained so high but it is a complex situation involving many factors and one that would repay intensive research.

Other factory conditions like lighting, ventilation and temperature were not the subject of annual statistical analysis as causes of accidents, though they have been systematically studied in England since 1917 under the direction of the Industrial Fatigue Research Board (later the Industrial Health Research Board). It has long been known that the conditions under which the body works affect productivity and accuracy; and that fatigue could be experienced if these conditions were adverse. It was also known that fatigue could be a prime cause of accidents. In 1943 Bartlett conducted some experiments on highly-skilled workers, and showed that fatigue could induce a man to mix his movements,[24] which in certain instances could cause an accident. As early as 1922 Osborne and Vernon showed the effect of temperature on workers, and that munition workers tended to have fewer accidents if the thermometer was around 67 degrees. Vernon, Bedford and Warner later showed that not only were accidents fewer at this temperature, but were less severe.[25] Humidity was another factor liable to lead to fatigue, though Eichna and others indicated that where men were acclimatized they could tolerate a high degree of humidity, even as much as a wet bulb temperature of 91 degrees, without losing efficiency. But if the temperature rose above 94 degrees they rapidly deteriorated.[26]

On the other hand, the famous Hawthorn experiment at the Western Electric Company, U.S.A., showed in 1946 that over a two-year period output increased if conditions like ventilation, rest pauses and shorter hours improved but, surprisingly, went on increasing when these improvements were gradually withdrawn. It would seem therefore that the response was not purely on the physiological plane but had an emotional element. It was suggested at Western Electric that the workers became interested in the experiment itself, that their relations with management had improved, and that it was not the conditions of work that made for higher productivity, but the knowledge of their own importance and status. How far this could be translated into the sphere of accident vulnerability would be another matter, and most likely a very different one.

Accident-proneness

After the war, H.M. Stationery Office reprinted the report of an inquiry made in 1926 into the 'human factor in the causation of accidents'.[27] This report was part of a series of inquiries, of which one by Osborne, Vernon and Muscio in 1922 had suggested that accidents were largely influenced by a special personal susceptibility inherent in the individual, and differing from one individual to another, and that workers do not start equal in their propensity to have accidents. It was found that the bulk of accidents was limited to a relatively small number of workers, three-quarters of those recorded having happened to one-quarter of the people exposed. Further research confirmed these findings, showing that, in almost all groups, the average number of accidents was much influenced by a comparatively small number of workers, and that the distribution among the workers was far from a chance one. It was also shown that if a person were predisposed in this way there was a tendency for him to suffer minor sicknesses more than others, and his accident-proneness was not limited to the factory, but was evident in the home as well. There was some indication that the tendency to suffer accidents decreased as a person got older, though correlation between greater experience and the number of accidents was lacking. Nor did there appear to be any sex difference in accident-proneness.

A further study of the matter was made by Dunbar in 1943,[28] who, while accepting the earlier findings, hazarded the additional information that an accident-prone subject could be recognized by his emotional instability and impulsiveness, his frequent failure to complete an educational programme, the turnover of his jobs, and an unstable home or family history. Hunter, in his book,[29] quoted two other supporting studies. One involved the psychological testing of 1,800 engineering apprentices to discover the degree of their neuro-muscular control and the examination of their subsequent records. The quarter with most impairment of function, as seen in their muscular precision, coordination of movement and ability to concentrate, had an accident rate two and a half times as high as that in the remaining three-quarters of the group. The second study took place in 1954[30] in the Nottinghamshire coalfield, when Whitfield was able to calculate the accident risk per shift for several moderately homogeneous working groups. From a comparison with the actual number of accidents it was clear that there were individual differences in accident susceptibility among these miners, a difference which persisted for several years. On closer analysis of three small samples, one of which was composed of miners with more accidents than the average, another with about the average number, and a third with fewer than the average, it was found that the younger accident-prone men were markedly deficient in the perceptual-cognitive tests, while the older ones showed impairment of motor control and coordination as compared with the individuals of similar ages in the other two samples. Whitfield suggested that a young accident-prone man was unable to appreciate the demands of a hazardous situation, and though capable of making the response, could not decide what to do. The older accident-prone man, on the other hand, could not make an adequate response, even though he saw the hazard and knew what to do.

Earlier studies had indicated that accident-proneness lessened with age, and Hunter faced this apparent paradox by suggesting that some accident-prone persons died young, others perhaps moved to less hazardous occupations, and others adjusted themselves to a reduced level of activity. This explanation would seem feasible. For if accident-proneness could indeed be the result of natural deficiency in motor ability, one would expect a deterioration with age rather than an improvement. Further research into the question seems necessary.

Some revulsion against the 'accident-prone' theory later made its appearance.[31] 'Accident-proneness,' it was said, 'is a rather hazy notion, and is far from being an unchangeable or permanent characteristic of the human personality. Are there not in any case certain speeds of work, working conditions and machines which induce accident-proneness? Is consideration given to the fatigue caused by overlong journeys between home and places of work, to the effect which the method of remuneration (bonuses for output, for dangerous work, etc.) may have on safety, to the muscular fatigue resulting from unusually heavy tasks, to the nervous fatigue produced by certain types of work requiring prolonged attention?'

The issue was examined again by scientists in Geneva,[32] but after a mathematical assessment of the probability of a worker sustaining an accident, they admitted that some workers had a larger number of accidents than others, and that an explanation other than mathematical probability had to be found. What this explanation could be was the problem. They emphasized that every accident was the coming together of a complex of circumstances, which, if they came singly or in a different arrangement, might not result in an accident at all. There would be the factors completely outside the mental processes of the injured worker, like the defective machine part, or the unsafe act of another person; there would be influences affecting a worker's outlook, like his domestic circumstances, his own age and experience. His own emotional condition at the time (the result of another complex of circumstances) would have to be taken into account – his being 'nervous' or 'calm', his wanting to take risks, to show his independence, his 'wanting to show off'. Moreover a second accident often resulted from an earlier one because he was expecting it, or had 'lost his nerve'. These and many other factors would have to be borne in mind in considering why some people tended to have more accidents than others.

The investigators laid stress on the possibility of change, that people could 'grow out' of the tendency, or conversely that there were so many varieties of work that people who have shown themselves liable to accidents in one type could be moved to another, where they were not a danger to themselves and others. Thus a crane-driver 'has not only to see how to pick up and transport a load, but also has to watch the movement of persons in the machine hall where he is working. If his mental constitution does not permit him to pay attention more or less simultaneously to a number of different things there will be a kind of accident-proneness that may result in accidents, not to himself, but to other persons'.[33] Such a person was not likely to 'grow out' of this difficulty, and the safest thing would be to move him to another job. The commentators did not acknowledge that deficiencies of this kind might be discovered before he was put on the crane, though one would have thought that enough tests had been devised to prevent bad selection of this sort. In fact, while there has been a tendency in some circles to denigrate the work of psychologists, it would seem just as unreasonable to dismiss their work out of hand, as to accept all their theories without question. That accident-proneness has a physio-psychological basis that is not easily changed would seem now to be reasonably well established.

REFERENCES

1. I.L.O. *Methods of Statistics of Industrial Injuries*. (Report prepared for the 6th International Conference of Labour Statisticians.) Montreal. 1947.

2. 1952 Chief Inspector of Factories Annual Report. p. 53. (1953–4 Cmd. 9154, xiii.)
3. Ibid.
4. 1954 Chief Inspector of Factories Annual Report. Cap. 4. (1955–6 Cmd. 9605, xvii.)
5. Ibid.
6. 1953 Chief Inspector of Factories Annual Report. p. 38. (1954–5 Cmd. 9330, v.)
7. Ibid. p. 39.
8. 1954 Factories Report. op. cit.
9. 1953 Factories Report. op. cit.
10. Ibid. p. 41.
11. Ibid.
12. 1954 Factories Report. op. cit.
13. Ibid.
14. Ibid.
15. T. A. Lloyd Davies, *The Practice of Industrial Medicine*. (Churchill, 1948.) p. 58.
16. *Industrial Accident Prevention*. National Joint Advisory Council. Industrial Safety Sub-Cttee. Report, Tables I and II; 1956 Non-Parl. Min. of Labour.
17. *Safety Review*. Vol 8. No. 4. April, 1959.
18. I.L.O. *Accident Prevention – A Workers' Manual*. Geneva, 1961. p. 23.
19. Ibid. p. 25.
20. Ibid. p. 20.
21. Ibid. p. 25.
22. Ibid. p. 4.
23. 1953 Factories Report. op. cit. p. 32.
24. *Proceedings of the Royal Society*. Series B. 131.
25. Industrial Health Research Board. Reports Nos. 19 and 39; 1922, 1927 Non-Parl.
26. *Journal of Industrial Hygiene and Toxicology*. Vol. 27, 1945
27. 1926 Industrial Health Research Board. No. 34.
28. T. A. Lloyd Davies. op. cit. p. 60.
29. D. Hunter, *Health in Industry*. Pelican, 1959. p. 84.
30. Ibid. p. 86.
31. Marcel Roberts, 'Industrial Accidents and their Prevention.' *International Social Service Review*. No. 7. October 1960.
32. I.L.O. *Accident Prevention*. op. cit. p. 100.
33. Ibid. p. 101.

2

INDUSTRIAL DISEASES

IT was early found that industry was responsible, not only for injuries to the workers, but also for certain diseases. Coal mining, for instance, was recognized as a cause of 'miners' pthisis' as it was then called, while certain types of match manufacturing gave rise to a deterioration of flesh and bone, called 'phossy jaw'. So, though the first Workmen's Compensation Acts and employers' liability legislation dealt mainly with injuries resulting from accidents, it was not long before a committee (1904) began to inquire into diseases, which could be traced back to industrial processes and activity as directly as could industrial accidents. The result of this was the introduction of new amending legislation culminating in the famous 1906 Workmen's Compensation Act. This extended the liability of employers to provide compensation in respect of certain diseases. Thereafter, a further committee was established to inquire, among other things, into the working of this part of the Act, and their findings may well be quoted here, as in spite of continuous efforts, particularly by the T.U.C., to alter the situation, the principles then laid down operated to the period of our inquiry.

There were three tests by which new diseases could be included in the benefit scheme.[1] Firstly, that they were outside the category of diseases already covered by the Act. Secondly, that the disease incapacitated the worker for more than a week, and thirdly, that the disease was so specific to the employment that it could be established as one peculiar to the trade, seldom appearing outside it. 'Many diseases may be regarded as trade diseases, because they are known to be specially prevalent among the workers in particular industries. But they may not be specific to the trade since they may frequently, though more seldom, attack persons engaged in other occupations, e.g. bronchitis is a trade disease among flax workers, a larger proportion of that class suffer from it than of other people; but it is not specific to the employment, for numbers of persons who are not flax workers contract it also. Thus, were bronchitis to be included as an industrial disease, it would attract endless litigation, as no one knows whether the sufferer has contracted it from dust irritation, or would have contracted it anyway, as hundreds of other people in the town do.'[2]

This had been the view of Parliament when the matter was debated in 1906. It was the view of the Gladstone Committee in 1907. It was again considered by the Holman Gregory Committee in 1920, who agreed with the contention. In 1932–3 a further Home Office departmental committee on compensation saw no reason to abandon it. When the new National Insurance (Industrial Injuries) Act was passed in 1946, it was evident that no change was contemplated. For in Section 55 (2) 'a disease may be prescribed if the Minister is satisfied that (*a*) it ought to be treated, having regard to its causes and incidence and any other relevant considerations, as a risk of the occupation, and not as a risk common to all persons; and (*b*) it is such that in the absence of special circumstances the attribution of particular cases to the nature of the employment can be established or presumed with reasonable certainty'.

While the principle has remained the same, the emphasis has clearly shifted. At the beginning, the test was that the disease was peculiar to the employment, and seldom appeared in other employments. By 1948 the test was that the disease could, with reasonable certainty, be traced back to the special circumstances of the employment, whether it appeared frequently in other occupations or not. Thus the disease of tuberculosis, though acquired by many people in different professions and trades, became a scheduled disease under the Act for nurses of T.B. patients, because, it was said, they were placed in a more vulnerable position than the population as a whole,

The old principle, with the new slant, was endorsed once more by a departmental committee under Mr. F. W. Beney, Q.C., which, in spite of three dissenting members, declared in 1955 that, in the present state of medical knowledge, there would be a serious danger of opening the door to unreasonable claims, if benefit were made available for disease under the same conditions as for accidents.

The principle itself has by no means gone unchallenged. The trade unions have been its implacable enemy, as may be read in successive government reports on the subject – particularly the Holman Gregory Report in 1920, and the Home Office departmental committee in 1932 and 1933. In the latter Sir Thomas Legge, medical adviser to the T.U.C., objected to the principle, because increasing medical knowledge made it possible to relate the cause of even some common ailments to occupational circumstances.[3] Though the committee agreed, they saw no reason to abandon the tests, because if the disease were common to the community, it would be difficult to prove that a particular employment was to blame. Further, they thought that widening the meaning in this way would put an unfair strain on employers, who were responsible for benefit under the workers' compensation law. The trade unions were not alone in their opposition. For, in March, 1947, a departmental committee under Judge Dale was appointed to review the policy of scheduling diseases in the light of modern industrial conditions. The report was published in November 1948, just four months after the Industrial Injuries Act came into force. Its recommendations were: that the old tests no longer applied, that an 'occupational disease' – a phrase more appropriate than 'industrial disease', should be defined as – 'any departure from health (other than accident) specific to the occupation, whether or no there is any special risk of exposure to it'. The committee were quite prepared to accept the system of 'presumptions', i.e. that some industries would be more likely to lead to certain diseases than others, but the system should not exclude diseases for which no presumption could be given. Thus the committee recommended that a scheduled disease should no longer be specific to the employment, all that was necessary was that it should be traced back to the occupation. Thus a person who caught a bad cold because he had to sit in a draught at work would, if this had become law, have been able to claim benefit under industrial injuries regulations. The Beney Committee sitting eight years later did not uphold these findings, and in consequence the meaning of the phrase 'prescribed disease' has not so far been radically altered.

A schedule of prescribed diseases has been drawn up, and is subject to review from time to time. Indeed the years since 1906 have been littered with resolutions from the T.U.C., and other bodies, recommending the addition of this or that disease to the schedule, and the recommendations of various government committees accepting or rejecting the proposals. The pressure, however, has not been in vain. For the evidence accumulated by interested bodies, and growing medical knowledge, have resulted in a substantial number of diseases (over forty) receiving recognition. To have the disease is not enough; proof of working in the prescribed industry, or with the prescribed poison (e.g. lead, manganese), or in prescribed occupations (e.g. twister's cramp if the person is employed in twisting cotton or woollen yarn) has also to be given. Since 1948 the Industrial Injuries Advisory Council has helped the Ministry in the make-up of the schedule. Thus in July 1958 a new schedule was drawn up consolidating all the diseases and occupations that had been added since the previous list was made ten years earlier.

The question of whether a person is suffering from one of these diseases is obviously a medical one, but it is one which has caused much criticism in the past. So much so that in 1935 a departmental committee of the Home Office (the Stewart Committee) was set up to go into the arrangements. At that time a worker had normally to get a certificate from the certifying factory surgeon that he was suffering from the disease. If either the worker or the employer was dissatisfied, appeal could be made to a medical referee. The Stewart committee, however, pointed out that certifying factory surgeons, though appointed by the chief inspector of factories, were, in the main, ordinary general practitioners, who could not be expected to know enough about industrial diseases to be in any way specialists. Especially was this so in the case of dermatitis produced by dust or liquids. Nevertheless, between 1933 and 1935 an average of 13,000 certificates per annum were given by these doctors. About 14 per cent of them went to appeal, and about 5½ per cent were allowed. Such figures would not suggest undue discontent with the findings of the certifying factory doctors, though many people shrink from querying the diagnosis of doctors, and the number of appeals might not be a yardstick of the prevalent disturbance. The Stewart committee mentioned other criticisms: that doctors in private practice were not always unbiased, and that there might be a danger of them divulging information to the other side (the employers, or the insurance company). Further, the certificate had to be obtained from the appropriate doctor in the district of employment, which might lead to hardship if the worker had moved to another district.

The medical referees, whose decision on appeal was final, were also usually private practitioners, though of consultant rank. The Home Office appointed about two hundred of them for England and Wales, and another eighty for Scotland. In some cases the appeal would be referred to the County Court, and the Judge had the right to appoint a medical referee to sit with him as assessor. Clearly on medical matters the Judge was obliged to accept his colleague's advice. So, in a sense, the medical referee became the sole judge on medical evidence whether he sat alone or with the Judge. This fact led to further criticism which had been thoroughly aired at the Holman Gregory inquiry sixteen years earlier. It had been said then that decisions of this sort should not be left to one man, who could not be expected to be infallible in such difficult cases; he might be biased on one side or the other; and, in any case, the fees for the work (two or three guineas) were insufficient to attract the men with most experience or the best qualifications. If, as often happened, he were asked to state the kind of job a man with one of the diseases was best fitted for, then the whole system was reduced to absurdity, as a medical consultant in private practice had obviously insufficient experience of industry to say.

The Stewart committee made far-reaching recommendations about appeals tribunals, medical advisory committees and the like. But the Second World War and the subsequent legislation prevented the specific proposals being implemented. All the same, the scheme that was ultimately set up under the National Insurance (Industrial Injuries) Act 1946 owed a great deal to the Stewart committee.

Two scheduled diseases departed from the normal system of ascertainment, pneumoconiosis and byssinosis. Pneumoconiosis is the generic name for a group of lung diseases caused by various kinds of dust found in industry. It has been defined in the Act as fibrosis of the lungs due to silica dust, asbestos dust or other dust, including the condition of the lungs known as 'dust reticulation'.

The three most important forms of the disease are silicosis, asbestosis and coal-workers' pneumoconiosis. Byssinosis occurs in workers in the cotton industry exposed to the inhalation of dust arising in the various processes. It is a respiratory complaint, bronchitic and asthmatic in type. It is slow in onset and may cause no disability for ten years or more. Later the disability increases until complete incapacity results. Provisions for these various lung and respiratory complaints were made piece-meal under the Workmen's Compensation Acts beginning with silicosis in 1918, and were added to as medical and industrial knowledge grew. After 1948 no distinction was made between the different forms of pneumoconiosis, but the scheme of benefit was limited to the specific occupations known to be at risk, though these could be added to from time to time.

However, in 1953 the Industrial Injuries Advisory Council recommended, and it was accepted in 1954, that the industrial injuries' benefits should be available to sufferers of pneumoconiosis from dusty occupations other than those in the schedule, provided that the claimant had been thus employed after July 5, 1948. Further, that while a schedule of occupations should be kept, and be added to only on proof that risk existed, the interpretation of occupational cover should be drawn in broad terms, rather than by reference to individual processes.

One aspect of the pre-1948 scheme of dealing with sufferers from pneumoconiosis was to withdraw them from their work in the mine. This was obviously a sensible precaution should the condition be infective, and was a safeguard against the exacerbation of the complaint in the sufferer. At least, these advantages were thought to exist. Other views, partly medical and partly economic, have since prevailed. In 1950, for instance, Dr. A. Meiklejohn writing in the *British Journal of Industrial Medicine* put a different point of view. 'No worker', he said, 'unless suffering from active T.B. should be suspended from his occupation in the mines'. To do so meant loss of self respect and status. Even work under 'approved conditions' in the mine was not the answer, because it was so hard to find, and because a man was best when working with his old mates in his old surroundings. The position was particularly serious for the man over forty, who could change his job only with the greatest difficulty. So, thought Dr. Meiklejohn, if it meant living dangerously for a time, the advantage of working up to capacity counter-balanced it. Of course such a man must be kept under constant medical review, in case his condition became active and a menace to others. But so long as he could, he should work, as work was the best corrective to an anxiety state. In the very next year (June 1951) a scheme was started to help the re-employment in coal mining of men suspended under the old workers' compensation schemes from such employment, because, it was stated, 'more medical knowledge, and experience of the social implications of the old scheme showed its limitations.'[4] While not in any way doubting the validity of these arguments, one cannot but reflect on the acute shortage of miners at that date.

Ascertainment of pneumoconiosis since the war has not been left to the ordinary medical boards, but has been dealt with by special panels in selected centres,* where highly qualified and experienced doctors were available. The scheme was not without its critics, amongst whom the National Union of Mineworkers was outstanding. In January 1959 they presented a comprehensive report to the T.U.C. on the assessment and diagnosis of the disease, as they were not satisfied that these had always been accurate. They recommended that general emphysema and chronic bronchitis, if they occurred with pneumoconiosis, should be included as industrial hazards. Further, there ought to be a right of appeal against the diagnosis itself, and special facilities should be available for autopsy in case of death from the disease, or what was suspected as the disease. These matters were submitted to the government for consideration.

One disease that has caused industry considerable trouble has been dermatitis. It was not compulsorily notifiable,† nor one which in all cases would attract industrial injuries benefit. Yet it has resulted in hardship to the individual, and has been one of the principal causes of lost time to industry. The Ministry of Labour has encouraged firms to volunteer information about the number of their cases, and has set up an advisory committee to give general help on the matter. No one has known the true incidence of the disease since, apart from the voluntary notification, only those claiming benefit were counted. Of the 2,093 notifications in 1957, the group of trades worst affected seemed

* Bristol, Cardiff, Edinburgh, Glasgow, London, Manchester, Newcastle, Sheffield, Stoke and Swansea were the centres in the years concerned.

† The T.U.C. recommended it should be.

to have been men in the metal manufacturing, engineering and allied industries.[5] When the M.P.N.I. made an estimate between June 1955 and June 1956, they found some 21,700 spells of incapacity had been due to it (17,500 males and 4,200 females), the average duration of each spell being thirty-eight days for men and fifty-one for women, a time-loss ratio of dermatitis to all other diseases of one to two for men, and three to four for women – a very disabling disease indeed. Medically, the causes of dermatitis would seem complex, ranging from the effect of certain materials like chemicals or oil, to the existence of physical agents like heat, cold and friction. A growing body of medical opinion has suggested personal rather than industrial causes; factors like nervous instability, emotional strain, faulty diet, poor physique, and certain abnormalities of the skin, were said to be predisposing agents. Prevention was clearly of vital importance, and industry was advised to take care in its selection of workers, so that those with predisposing factors were not exposed to risk, and should irritants appear in the manufacturing processes, to have them removed, or provide constant attention so that harm would be minimized.

1956 Survey of the Pottery Industry

In February 1956 the Ministry of Labour announced a pilot survey of the pottery industry; a survey of which the main objects were to examine the health hazards in the industry, to see what diseases troubled it, and how the health of the worker was supervised. The pottery industry was chosen because it was not too large, it was mainly concentrated in one area (Stoke-on-Trent), and because the size of the units varied. It was an old industry with considerable health hazards, which had been tackled resolutely for many years. The report covered 298 factories employing over 48,000 workers (19,000 males, 29,000 females). It was thus a largely female-employing industrial sample, of which nearly 2,000 were part-time and over 2,000 under eighteen years old.

It was found that in spite of the Pottery Regulations, dating back to 1913, the chief disease was still 'Potter's Rot' (pneumoconiosis), and the chief hazard continued to be dust. A constant battle was being waged in each factory against the menace, by the use of non-poisonous materials, dust extractors, dust control and the promotion of cleanliness in the person himself, and his clothing. But the battle was uneven, owing to the small size of some of the factories, and the fact that many of the units were old. Thus the installation of modern equipment, and the effective oversight of all the factors involved were more difficult in some works than in others. Moreover, the system of works' inspectors (the appointment of workmen to see that the regulations were carried out), had not worked very well since the war.

Lead poisoning on the other hand had been practically wiped out. Whereas over 200 cases were notified in 1900, there had been none since 1952. This was due to changes in the methods of working and in the materials used, such as the replacement of soluble lead oxides by relatively insoluble lead compounds in the making of glazes. Dermatitis was found to be a hazard in this industry, especially in the processes involving the use of solvents, friction, or the handling of wet materials. Cleanliness and the use of barrier cream were the best preventives, but it was not always easy to persuade the workers to use cream on their hands.

The value of the survey lay in the attention it focused on the special hazards of the industry and the way it stimulated the individual firms to press on with safety and preventive measures.* It did not make any new discoveries, or provide a new way of assessing the amount of disease, a matter of some difficulty as the following section will show.

Amount of notifiable industrial disease

Crude figures on the number of persons afflicted by industrial disease need to be read with caution. For instance in 1947 there was an overall increase of 20 per cent over the 1939 figures. The total number of gassing cases had risen by a third, while deaths from pneumoconiosis showed an 80 per cent increase. Even the number of dermatitis cases notified had increased by two-thirds. The chief factory inspector in his report in 1947 commented on the apparent deterioration by pointing to the difficulties of making precise comparisons between the two dates. Medical knowledge had changed, more was known, and more had been found out about the nature and causes of the various diseases, with their

* In 1962 a joint standing committee for the pottery industry was appointed.

occupational history and social background. Firms were more conscious of the effects of occupational hazards upon health, and more ready to report illness than before. Many diseases were more easily identified, e.g. epitheliomatous ulceration was more easily diagnosed in the early wart stage and could be cured before it became cancerous. Crude numbers could also be affected because cases were referred to the doctor in their early stages, allowing better diagnosis and prognosis. Further, the increase in the working population and the number fully employed were material factors affecting the general picture. Even in pneumoconiosis, with the apparent serious increase in deaths, improved diagnosis could ascribe deaths to this cause, which would not have been so numbered in the past. Therefore comparisons were misleading.

However, it has to be admitted that, in the years after 1948, there was not an appreciable reduction in the number of industrial diseases notified; and the deaths from pneumoconiosis and byssinosis have shown a distinct increase[6] (in 1953 there were 2,055 deaths in England and Wales rising to 2,201 in 1962). Apart from coal mining, pottery was the most vulnerable industry for this disease, though stone quarrying and the shaping of stone by masons were also risky.

As for the time lost to industry through disease, the amount was by no means negligible. It was well over one and a quarter million days in 1954, and though this had gone down, it was still over a million in 1961. Compared with time lost through accident (over 18,000,000 days per year) perhaps diseases were not such a threat to the stability of industry. But the crucial factor for industry was not the number of workers who contracted diseases but the time lost per man. A workshop unit would manage to keep going with a man short, if his absence was only for a few days, but when he was away for several weeks a major reorganization would be required. This was difficult enough in large factories, able to afford alternative operatives, either by employing more labour temporarily, or having more than one worker trained to do a particular job, but in small firms no stand-in of this sort would be possible, and the absence of even one person for a prolonged period would be a serious embarrassment. Thus while the average duration of an accident could vary between fourteen and thirty-one days, for a disease the range might be anything from nineteen to fifty-seven days.

There appeared to be a pronounced sex difference in this matter, for females required more time than males. In diseases their average absence was half as long again as for males. In 1960 the average duration of disease for females was forty-six days and for males thirty-one days. No adequate explanation of this discrepancy has yet been put forward, as one would not suppose that the prescribed diseases suffered by women were any more serious than those for men. It may be that the circumstances of female employment and their domestic arrangements induced the doctors to insist on longer periods of recuperation before signing them fit to work. Or perhaps females did not seek advice as early as males, necessitating longer periods of sick leave when they did succumb. Whatever the explanation, the total amount of time lost by females was only a fraction of the time lost by males, since many fewer women were at risk.*

* e.g. through diseases alone in 1960 males lost 890,000 days, females 300,000 days.

REFERENCES

1. *Compensation for industrial diseases*. Dept. Cttee. Report; 1932 Non-Parl. Home Office.
2. *Workmen's Compensation*. Cttee. (Holman Gregory, Ch.). Report. Part III. (1920 Cmd. 816, xxvi.)
3. *Compensation for industrial diseases*. 1932 Report. op. cit.
4. 1952 Chief Inspector of Factories Annual Report. (1953–4 Cmd. 9154, xiii.)
5. 1957 Industrial Health. Chief Inspector of Factories Annual Report. (1957–8 Cmnd. 558, xiii.)
6 Chief Inspector of Factories Annual Reports.

3

ACCIDENT PREVENTION

ONE of the most carefully prepared, though in some of its conclusions curiously 'dated', government reports of the twentieth century was the Holman Gregory Report on workmen's compensation published in 1920. In its two years of work this departmental committee investigated many angles of the industrial injury problem, and early recognized that compensation for injury and the prevention of accidents were two branches of industrial legislation that travelled along separate lines.

This dichotomy developed late in the nineteenth century. For when employers' liability legislation had first been considered in the middle of the century, it had aimed at securing greater protection for the workman's life and limb, as well as compensation for those injured by industrial accident. It was argued, for instance, that if accidents could be made costly to the employer, he would be obliged to take steps to avoid them. Indeed, as far back as 1846, the select committee on railway labourers,[1] shocked by the casualties among 200,000 navvies engaged in the work of railway construction, reported in favour of making railway companies pay compensation for accidents, and the power of the purse as an incentive to accident prevention. A similar idea was voiced at the T.U.C. in 1877 by Thomas Holliday, a miners' leader, who wanted 'preservation of our lives and bodies' by making employers pay the cost of accidents. His aim was not so much the money, but the means of accident prevention. Again, in 1893, the Home Secretary, when moving a second reading of the Employers' Liability Bill, attacked Mr. Chamberlain's amendment favouring general workers' compensation, on the grounds that employers could insure against monetary loss, and that this would negative any incentive there might have been to exercise greater care for the safety of the workers.

In spite of the voices raised to encourage preventive action, the Employers' Liability Acts at that time came to be thought of as a way of supporting an injured man and his family during incapacity, or compensating for his death, while the prevention of accidents was furthered through the development of factory and workshop law and the mines' regulations and Acts.

In America, the Holman Gregory Committee pointed out, this was not so. In that country various incentive systems were introduced and found to be successful. For instance, there was 'merit-rating', where employers, who took all reasonable precautions against accidents, were rewarded by being able to pay smaller premiums. Or 'schedule rating', where the insurance company sent round an inspector to award credit, if preventive measures like hand-rails, guards on machinery, etc., had been adopted by the employer, or debit, if they had not, the net premium being calculated on a plus or minus schedule. Or 'experience rating', where smaller premiums were exacted, if a firm could show, over a number of years, that it had fewer accidents than other similar firms.

'Experience rating' or 'special rating' as it was called, was not uncommon in Britain, especially in favour of large firms, who could claim reduced rates of premium if the number of accidents had been few. But this involved no systematic inspection, no credit because safety precautions had been taken, or because a positive effort to promote safety through safety committees or other means had been inaugurated. Further the 'no claims bonus' might be lost through a single serious accident, which might not be the fault of the employer at all. In any case such a bonus was criticized because in practice it tended to benefit the big firms and not the small ones.

One of the deputy chief inspectors of factories (Mr. Gerald Bellhouse, C.B.E.), invited by the Holman Gregory Committee to give evidence, declared himself strongly in favour of 'schedule rating', and advocated the establishment of a central body under the state to fix standards for different trades. All occupiers who complied with these standards should then be given credit on a specified scale. Provided that insurance companies were represented, the factory department consulted, and employers given the right of appeal to an independent tribunal in any case of dispute, he thought the system would work, and there would be no difficulty between it and the enforcement of the Factories Acts. The committee thought well of this scheme, especially as it was supported by the Accident Offices Association. However, it has never been seriously considered by the legislature, any more than has any other financial incentive towards safety. Instead, Parliament has relied on the Factories Acts and on persuasion and appeals to firms to improve their safety precautions in the interests of public relations; or, in times of stress, and in a few instances, on naked force, as in the Factories (Medical & Welfare Services) Order 1940 which imposed a statutory obligation in munition and other government factories to employ medical supervision.

State effort

A review of the various preventive methods operating during the period is confused by the lack of clear-cut precision in the State's function. That persuasion rather than force should be the criterion became overt government policy in November 1958, when Mr. Iain Macleod, then Minister of Labour, was moving the second reading of the Factories Bill. He was quoted in *The Times* as saying: 'The stage has probably been reached where compulsion is not always the best method of proceeding. The voluntary method of dealing with safety, health and welfare will, for the first time, have a statutory basis. Clause 19 puts the obligation on the Minister to promote safety, health and welfare by the collection and dissemination of information, and by assisting with investigations.'[2]

Nevertheless, in spite of the non-compulsory nature of much of the government's action, a vitally important area of power rested in their hands by the operation of the various Factories Acts.

(*a*) *The Factory Inspector*

The spearhead of the government's attack was undoubtedly the factory inspector, whose duty it was to see that the Factories Acts were honoured; they have always been pioneers in preventing injuries to workers. Their functions have been five-fold: (*a*) to inspect and approve the health and safety of the workplace; (*b*) to promote the health, welfare and safety of the worker, and to see that the regulations were carried out; (*c*) to see that machinery and processes had adequate guards if they were dangerous; (*d*) to ensure that the law concerning the hours of work for women and juveniles was not evaded; (*e*) in the event of an accident or mishap resulting in the death of the worker, or his absence from work for more than three days, to visit the works and take appropriate action.

To accomplish this exacting and highly expert job a small band of factory inspectors, employed by the Ministry of Labour, have struggled to keep an eye on what was going on in the factories themselves. To illustrate the magnitude of their task, figures for 1957 may be quoted.[3] The actual number of inspectors was 388, and the number of factories to be visited was 225,937. Of these 72,023 were 'on priority', of which about 71 per cent were visited during the year. Of the much greater number not 'on priority' only 36 per cent were visited. Thus more than half the registered factories were not visited at all during the period.

It had long been recognized that the number of factory inspectors was grossly inadequate. For instance in 1926 an international labour convention, adopted by Great Britain, provided for annual visits to every factory. This has never been possible. Somewhat later (1930) a departmental committee in this country recommended that all important factories should be visited annually, and the rest every alternate year, and that every factory should be thoroughly inspected not less than every four years. But with the average number of inspectors since the war being in the region of 350 (there were 447 by 1963), and the number of factories to be inspected approximately 250,000, such an aspiration was absurdly wide of the mark. The problem was not confined to this country. For although Great Britain appeared to have a substantially lower rate of inspectors to workers employed than a number of other European countries,[4] a post-war (1947) international labour convention was obliged to lower its sights from those of twenty years earlier, and require 'inspections to be as often and as thorough as is necessary to ensure the effective application of legislation'; and the United Kingdom ratified this. However, even this somewhat vague requirement was not always achieved[5] as, of the 60,000 to 70,000 factories on the 'priority' list, seldom more than three out of four were visited during 1955–7 while, of the rest, just over one in three were seen.* The position was eased later as a result of the White Paper on *Staffing and organisation of the factory inspectorate* (1956), which recommended a considerable increase in personnel, especially in the chemical and engineering branches, and for building sites. It was, however, one thing to increase the establishment and another to recruit suitable staff. By 1958 there was still a 10 per cent gap between the number allowed and the number actually in posts (viz.: 443:409). In 1963 the cadre of the inspectorate was increased to 477, but even counting acceptable candidates, there were thirty vacancies.

The success of this devoted little band of men and women has been hard to assess. They worked mainly by advice, exhortation and warning. Without them, there were grounds for fearing that firms would have been more lax than they were. It has been impossible to produce evidence in support of this impression, since by its very nature statistical corroboration was not available. The annual number of prosecutions of erring firms was a poor guide, as the cases were instituted most unwillingly, either as a last resort against the recalcitrant occupier on whom warnings had no effect, or where an accident had occurred as a result of such serious neglect that no employer could remain unchallenged. In 1962, for instance, the total number of 'informations' laid was 1,695 and the number of convictions 1,603, while the total fines amounted to nearly £39,000. This was a very small number compared with the total of firms visited, and was clearly concerned with but a minority of the matters found to be defective on inspection. An analysis of the figures revealed that over half the convictions were concerned with faults in safety precautions (1,112), of which inadequate fencing of machinery and insufficient precautions against falling from heights were outstanding. The only other group of offences at all numerous was that concerned with 'health' (207), in which some default over medical examination was the chief factor. Nor was the annual fluctuation of prosecutions at all significant, as it varied from a little above the 2,000 mark in some years, to a little below 1,000 in others. What was significant was the large percentage of successful convictions (more than 90 per cent of 'informations'), and the size of the

* 'Seen' does not necessarily mean a full inspection.

average fine (under £20), matters which will be dealt with more fully in the final chapter.

The accident rate might have been some measure of the inspectors' effectiveness, if accidents could have been reduced to a simple formula. As this was not possible, we are left with the general and widely-held opinion that, were the number of qualified inspectors greater, the safety and welfare of British industry would have improved.

(b) The Medical Factory Inspector

So far we have discussed only the 'general purpose' factory inspector. There were included in the number some experts, such as those specializing in the electrical, engineering and chemical branches of industry. Of particular interest were the medical inspectors, because theirs was a task concerned so largely with prevention. Indeed it might be said that their main *raison d'être*, along with appointed factory doctors and the medical staff of the factories, was to anticipate anything likely to be injurious to health, and to use every means to prevent it. In a sense, they were more concerned with research into the industrial arrangements leading to an accident or a disease, than in evaluating the medical circumstances of an injured man himself.

Administration of the medical element in industry was partly statutory* and partly voluntary. The statutory side included the engagement of 'appointed factory doctors', who have become the backbone of the scheme. For, though they have been part-time, and mainly general practitioners, there were enough of them (1,561 in 1962) to cover the country reasonably well. As their chief purpose was to examine young workers under eighteen, all workers in unhealthy employment, and to investigate anyone suffering from a notifiable industrial disease, they were obviously in a strong position to give advice to the medical inspectors, and to draw attention to points of vulnerability. The role of the medical inspectors themselves was of great importance since, being full-time and concerned with a region or the country as a whole (the establishment included one medical inspector for each

* In 1844 a 'certifying surgeon' had to examine young entrants to industry to certify that they were nine years old or over. It was not until 1898 that a 'medical inspector' was added to the factory inspectorate. By 1937 the certifying surgeon, whose duties had been enlarged with the years, became the 'examining surgeon', and in 1948 an amending Act changed his title to that of 'appointed factory doctor'.

of the fourteen divisions, and five at headquarters), they were in a position to see the picture in the round. By training and experience they were well equipped to help in the dissemination of medical knowledge on industrial questions, and to advise their more local colleagues (appointed factory doctors, and industrial doctors) on difficulties that cropped up from time to time. They were also strategically placed to carry out research on aspects of industrial health, an activity that was officially encouraged by the Factories Act, 1961, though inspectors have been engaged in it for years.

As for the work of the appointed factory doctors, there has been very little published information. The one group of statistics that has given a glimpse at a limited field of their work concerned the medical examination of young workers. This was clearly an important function, as those young people who had somehow escaped the net of the school medical service, might be picked up at this point and either refused a permit to work, or given only a provisional one. It said something for the school medical service and the national health service in general, that in 1962 out of over half a million examinations, only 1,529 were given outright rejections, or just over 0·2 per cent; a further 25,000 were given either provisional or conditional certificates. Of those rejected more than twice as many girls as boys failed to pass, though if the number suffering from pediculosis were subtracted, the numbers of boys and girls rejected were about equal. The chief cause of trouble among the rest seemed to have been 'refractive errors' in the eyes; three out of eight rejected young people had this difficulty. Epilepsy and skin trouble were the only other major ills, though a trickle of nervous, circulatory and other illnesses appeared in the records.

Voluntary effort

In 1951 a committee investigated the work of the industrial health services, but forbore to comment on the value of the statutory provision, preferring, it would seem, to save their remarks for the voluntary provision by individual firms. The fact that many firms appointed their own doctors and nurses was to them a sign of good management, and evidence of the fulfilment of a moral obligation to the workers. The function of these voluntarily provided industrial medical officers was described as: (*a*) the giving of general advice to management on industrial hazards, safety precautions, cause and prevention of industrial disease; (*b*) the examination of individual workers to see whether they were suitable for certain jobs, or, if exposed to occupational risks, were in good health; (*c*) the supervision of the therapeutic services, first aid and medical care in the factory; (*d*) health education among all personnel. The committee concluded with the remark that 'these services, which may now be regarded as a normal function of enlightened management, are important to industry by reason of the contribution they make both to the health of the workers, and to productivity. They help to ensure that the worker is at least no worse in health as a consequence of his work, and may ensure that he is better'.[6] Further, they pointed out that 'the services lessen the demand on the national health service, principally by preventing the occurrence of accidents and disease, but also by giving immediate and easily available treatment to minor injuries, which if neglected, either from ignorance, apathy or a disinclination to lose working time, may lead to serious complications at a later stage'.

While larger firms were providing their own medical arrangements,* the position of the smaller firms gave cause for concern. As nearly a quarter of a million firms employed fewer than fifty workers, it would be clearly impossible for each of them to develop a full-time medical department. Yet, accident, disease, and ordinary sickness might strike anywhere. It seemed all the more desirable, therefore, that co-operative schemes should be developed. Pioneer work had already shown what could be done, as in the Slough industrial health service, and that at Hillington, each covering more than 100 firms, and the Bridgend one which was a joint scheme for about forty factories. In these cases really modern medical departments with full-time staff were kept in existence by the enlightened self-interest of the firms, whose proximity made a joint arrangement viable. In July 1960, the Nuffield Foundation, stimulated by the need for further experiment, gave £250,000 to extend group industrial health services. By 1961 Rochdale had begun a pilot scheme, and in the following year Dundee was developing another.† It is difficult to understand

* In 1951 nearly 4,000 full-time industrial nurses were employed (mainly S.R.N.).

† By 1963 other group industrial health schemes were developing notably at West Bromwich and Manchester.

why the growth of new 'trading estates', in the inter-war and post-war period, did not encourage the creation of group industrial health centres, and why their development has had to depend on the benevolence of a charitable trust.

No accurate or comprehensive survey was made of the voluntary medical services supplied by firms, so the exact number and qualifications of the personnel and the scope of their functions have remained unknown. But in 1955 and again in 1958 the medical department of the factory inspectorate conducted small surveys whose results may be found in the appropriate reports.[7] In one, the medical inspectors allowed themselves to stray from the statistical information to give their own impressions of the importance attached to the medical officer's functions in the factory, and to summarize management's views on the medical services.

The management in some firms, apparently, saw no advantage at all in having a medical department. But of those who did, the point most stressed was that it helped to save time for the workers, because they could get treatment at the factory instead of having to take time off to go to their own doctor, or the hospital. Some (but only a few) thought the presence of a medical department promoted good health. Nearly as important was the view that the morale of the workers was improved, because they felt more confidence in the goodwill of the management. Also, it gave workers an opportunity to take personal problems to the doctor. Of much less importance, in management's estimation, was the research function of the industrial medical team, though managers in some of the larger works did allow that it could give advice on working conditions, and on health hazards inherent in the processes of the firm. The doctor's place in rehabilitation was seldom mentioned, and few considered it at all important for him to fulfil any non-industrial health function (e.g. on joint consultation committees).

As for the workers' attitude to medical supervision in the factory, we have to go to another survey[8] where the comment was laconic. Few, it seems, ever gave it a thought. None saw it as a means of giving advice on positive industrial health. But withal there was very little hostility to the schemes!

First Aid

It was not until the Factories Act of 1937 that first-aid boxes were a requirement in all factories. Before that, the obligation was limited to certain works, specified under the Police, Factories, etc. (Miscellaneous Provisions) Act, 1916, and the Workmen's Compensation Act, 1923. The habit of providing emergency medical equipment had been growing, and the First Aid in Factories Order, 1938, merely accelerated the movement, and provided it with standards. It was laid down in the Order that boxes should contain certain articles, and that factories should make sure that someone on the staff could use them and would have access to them. The actual number of workers dictated, to some extent, what was provided, the general principle being, the larger the staff and the more dangerous the process, the higher should be the standard of first-aid provision.

Two factors have conspired to render the 1938 Order obsolescent: (*a*) experience that its application has been haphazard, and in many cases unsatisfactory; and (*b*) the change in medical opinion itself about the efficiency of certain methods and medicaments.

But it is to the factory inspectorate that we owe most in bringing to light the true state of affairs. For in September 1955 the department initiated a small pilot survey into the industrial health of a fairly typical northern town. Nearly half the 760 factories were concerned with textiles, or with engineering and metal goods, and nearly 30,000 workers were employed. Most of the factories were small, with fewer than twenty-five workers, but many factories manufactured food or drink and were therefore keenly health conscious, and aware of the need for cleanliness to promote purity in the product. On the other hand some of the works were old and the processes dirty and, without expensive structural alterations, were not conducive to the maintenance of high health standards.

Under the 1938 Order, standards of 'good', 'satisfactory' and 'unsatisfactory' were laid down for first-aid boxes, and first-aid arrangements in general. 'Good' was applied where additional facilities to the minimum required by the Order were present, e.g. if means were available, and in use, for cleansing the hands of the first-aid officer, and the skin of the injury. 'Satisfactory' meant that the facilities available were clean, and the technique for treating minor injuries had included cleanliness. The rest were 'unsatisfactory'.

When the 760 factories were subjected to the survey, 43 were 'good', 450 were found to be 'satisfactory', and 267 'unsatisfactory' in their first-aid arrangements. Unfortunately, this latter category would have been even larger had a rigid adherence to the letter of the standards been observed. For instance, had they insisted on the contents of the box being aseptic, many more would have had to be counted 'unsatisfactory'. Accordingly, they were ready to pass the box if it was clean, and if the techniques of treating minor illnesses included cleanliness. The standard 'unsatisfactory' was therefore pitched low, and can be illustrated by the following description, which apparently was repeated many times in the reports of the various inspectors:

'The box, which would err on the side of dirtiness rather than scrupulous cleanliness, would contain an assortment of roller bandages, a partially used open roll of surgical lint, the outer layer or two of which would be decidedly dirty, and a partially used roll of adhesive plaster, and a tourniquet. A few sterilized wound and burn dressings in the various prescribed sizes would probably be available, some opened. Almost certainly there would be a reasonable stock of adhesives for wound dressings, with an even chance that they would be in the form of a continuous strip dressing, and not as individual dressings. A choice of antiseptics would be provided. Eye-drops, commonly in two varieties labelled "factory eye-drops No. 1" and "factory-eye drops No. 2", and sal-volatile would also most likely be present. A bottle of aspirin tablets, patent cough mixture, and probably a record of treatments, but no instructions on how to carry them out.' It was also remarked that in many factories a strategic reserve of roller bandages, adhesive plaster, lint and sterilized dressings would be kept locked up 'because they tended to disappear if left available'. In all classes of factory, there was a marked dislike of small sterile finger dressings in the treatment of minor injuries, because, it was said, they soiled so easily and were clumsy. Instead, they preferred a piece of lint, medicated with antiseptic, and fixed with an adhesive dressing.

This state of affairs naturally raised the question of whether the incidence of sepsis was high in the town's factory accidents. The records of three years 1953–5 were scrutinized and some 10 per cent of reportable accidents did mention sepsis, which was 3 per cent higher than the national average. However the whole of the region had a high sepsis incidence, so it would be unwise to read too much into these figures. Moreover none can tell whether the sepsis was acquired at the factory, or crept in during home treatment.

The provision of a first-aid box is one thing, someone trained and available to use it is another. There was a distinct indication in this survey that training was not up to standard. In 60 per cent of the factories management had given little, if any, thought to training in first aid. It was a matter of luck if anyone happened to be there who was trained. Even the ones who had had some tuition had nearly always obtained it years ago, and therefore were unaware of modern methods. In factories employing over fifty workers (the only ones obliged to have trained personnel) the standard of training of first-aid workers was found to be lamentably low. Many more were rated 'unsatisfactory' than 'good' or 'satisfactory'. In the face of this accumulation of evidence, it is not difficult to understand why the report advocated an improvement in the general standard of first-aid.

The findings of this survey were not the only straws in the wind. For, since the outbreak of war, medical views on first-aid treatment have changed. For instance, the presence of antiseptics has led to their being used undiluted on wounds, sometimes to the injury of the surrounding body area. The cocaine eye-drops have been criticized, because by anaesthetizing the eye, they have tended to mask symptoms of injury, causing delay in acquiring skilled treatment. Thus the time was ripe for change.

It was to the credit of the department concerned that by 1960 a new First-Aid Boxes in Factories Order came into operation, and a standard of equipment was laid down applying to factories of every size. Further, in the Factories Act, 1959, power was given to prescribe the standards of training required by the responsible first-aid worker in factories employing over fifty workers. The position of the smaller factory has been left for the time being as before, except that the so-called 'responsible person' would be in charge of a box whose contents were as good as that of the biggest factory. On the other hand, an intensive persuasion campaign was launched to achieve better standards of training among all first-aid workers, whatever the size of the factory. The position did not satisfy everyone and, among others, the T.U.C. recommended that up-to-date training should be obligatory for first-aid personnel in factories of whatever size, if the nature of the work was at all hazardous. As this was similar to a recommendation made by an inter-departmental committee in 1937 it cannot be said the government has been over-hasty or impetuous.

Accident Services

First aid in the factory could be only one stage in preventing more serious results from accidents. Another would be the adequacy of hospital provision. For by quick and highly-skilled treatment many a man could be back at work in a few days where, without it, he might be crippled for life.

Awareness of this has given rise to a demand for a specialized 'accident service', involving mobile operating theatres, special 'fracture clinics' in suitably-placed hospitals, and a highly-trained mobile team of skilled personnel. The demand was first formulated by the British Medical Association in 1935 and, in consequence, the following year, an inter-departmental committee was set up to consider the issue.[9] On the whole the committee agreed with the B.M.A. and suggested that as treatment for fractures in the ordinary hospital wards was not adequate, special departments for the purpose should be established in the larger hospitals, each with a surgeon in charge, and having nurses, physiotherapists and an almoner's department to see that the right treatment was available, and that cases were followed-up on leaving hospital.

While rehabilitation for disablement has become an important social service through the recommendations of a subsequent committee,[10] the idea of a 'fracture clinic' was allowed to lie until the British Orthopaedic Association once again raised the matter in 1959 and received much publicity. The problem, they said, was much larger than factory accidents alone. For 'on average forty-five people die from accidents every day, five from accidents at work, sixteen travelling, and twenty-four from injuries in their home'.[11] The problem was large, but it was not large enough to justify the establishment of expensive accident clinics in every hospital. Thus, even in London, where there were more than 100 casualty-receiving hospitals, few received enough casualty cases to warrant an efficient twenty-four-hour service, nor were they fully equipped or properly staffed to do so. In many, according to the report, the casualty officer had to leave at five o'clock in the evening, and his work thereafter was delegated to a junior house surgeon, who had other duties. It was clearly a national problem, and the report strongly recommended that the government should consider it as such, and that regional hospital boards and teaching hospitals should be authorized to create at least one comprehensive accident depot within each area. There was a further comment from an eminent London casualty surgeon about the lack of planning in the London area. 'The ambulance service is efficient,' he said, 'but delay is often caused by patients being transferred from one hospital to another, due to lack of liaison and an organized service. The present system is responsible yearly for much gross inhumanity to patients, much medical inefficiency, and a great deal of additional expense.'[12]

Informal effort to implement the B.O.A's suggestion followed, particularly to plan a two-pronged service that would serve the whole country. The idea of a double service was not new, having been recommended by Government Committees in 1937 and in 1951,[13] but it was re-examined to see whether a well-staffed, well-equipped hospital could be strategically sited in each region, and whether 'peripheral hospitals', less well equipped, could be 'receiving centres' for the localities, to which a 'flying squad' of highly-skilled medical personnel could be sent from the central hospital, and to which patients might go for recuperation. It was thought that the whole scheme would cost an extra £100 millions a year (according to the money values of the 'fifties). Mr. Seddon,[14] the then president of B.O.A., said that, at one accident centre, the attendance time of patients with minor accidents had been reduced, since the service began, from an average of three weeks to five days. If, by setting up other centres, there could be a similar saving of time, the expenditure would be well worth it, since, apart from the lessening of human suffering and frustration, output would increase and the productivity of industry would rise. A year later a standing committee of medical personnel was formed to review the accident services, and the B.M.A. issued a pamphlet entitled *The future of occupational health services*, advocating the establishment of a central occupational health service council, supported by regional councils.

Meanwhile pressure of another sort was directed at the government as a result of the 1959 Factories Act, under which the Minister of Labour had a duty to promote research into the safety of premises and machinery in industry and to disseminate information on health, safety and welfare to occupiers of factories. The Industrial Health Advisory Committee (I.H.A.C.), already established by the Minister, was given additional power and urgency, and one of the lines they pursued was an inquiry into the need for more chemical, physical, and biological testing, to reduce health risks in factories. This led the B.M.A. and the T.U.C. to make a joint approach to the Prime Minister asking for a properly-equipped industrial health laboratory service in place of the small department that was spending only a few hundreds a year. The result of the approach was negative at the time. The T.U.C., however, went further (and were joined in their challenge by the I.L.O.) and asked for a comprehensive occupational health service, similar to that set up in the north of England in 1959 by the Nuffield Trust and the department of Industrial Health, King's College, Newcastle upon Tyne. But the government was unwilling to consider this idea either,[15] and referred them to the government schemes of rehabilitation and training, and to the British national health service, which was said to supply the bulk of the medical and nursing services required. The matter was not allowed to rest here, and by 1963 the Minister of Health was able to announce that the hospital plan for the next ten years included the establishment of a fully-equipped accident unit in every major hospital in the country. The simultaneous pressure from many directions had thus succeeded in promoting a new approach to the accident provision of Britain.

Safety Promotion

That a great deal of statutory and voluntary effort was at work in industry and the medical profession, must already be evident from the foregoing. It remains now to assess two other aspects which, if sincerely promoted by workers and employers, would go a long way to reduce the number of accidents at work. They are: training for safety, with or without the appointment of safety officers, and the work of accident prevention committees.

Training for Safety

Safety is clearly the responsibility of management, and to meet their obligations many firms had appointed 'safety officers' whose duty it was to see that all prescribed safety measures were in use, whether guards on machinery, clear passage ways, measures against fire-risks, safety clothing, detecting faults in the fabric of the building or dangers in the materials used. These men might be full-time or part-time, though where buildings were extensive, or there were dangers in the processes themselves, the purpose of his work could only be adequately achieved where a man spent his whole time on the job. No figures have been made available of the total numbers of these officers, but as pressure for greater safety grew, it seemed the number designated for this work tended to increase.

In spite of the appointment of safety watchdogs, accidents occurred because there was no short-cut to safety. Unless safety could become the concern of every human being in industry, the unhappy toll of maiming, disease and death was bound to continue. So it all came back to training and research. Reference has already been made to management's obligation to train the young and the new recruit in how to use machinery safely, and to the disastrous results if this duty were neglected. Training in safety was seen to be necessary for other ranks too, particularly supervisors and the managers themselves. To help in this many organizations took a hand. The Birmingham Industrial Training Centre at Acocks Green was established in 1951 to train local foremen and supervisory staff in safety measures. Its doors were open to similar staff from different parts of the country. Safety was taught locally by 'Training Within Industry' (T.W.I.) methods. Information could be obtained from such bodies as the Royal Society for the Prevention of Accidents, the British Safety Council, as well as the *ad hoc* safety committees set up by individual industries. The Ministry of Labour itself was active, both through its own staff, and its publications. There was, in fact, no lack of information, or opportunities for training in safety; what was lacking was the systematic and continuous use of safety measures and priorities through a lifetime of work by each individual.

Training and propaganda were necessary and so was research.

For unless there could be a constant effort so to improve machinery that safety was built into it, or the study of workshop conditions produced an arrangement where falls, or the possibility of being struck by an object, became exceptional, then avoidable accidents would continue to happen. Nor should psychological factors be omitted. For personnel should be carefully sorted out to keep the 'accident-prone' out of danger, and to fit the worker into the most suitable job. Once again there was no lack of agencies, from the Department of Scientific & Industrial Research to the research departments of machinery-making firms; from the Universities and Technical Colleges to the safety departments of individual companies. There is no doubt that machines were much safer as a result, that the conditions in which people worked were healthier, that the thought and care put into workshop architecture have made the workplace safer. It was all the more disappointing, therefore, that the number of industrial injuries was not reduced, especially among the young.

The Safety Committee

The real hope lay in the people themselves, in the all-out co-operative effort of management and workers to acquire an ingrained habit of safety-mindedness. The national joint advisory committee in their 1956 report on accident prevention postulated six principles of accident prevention.[16] They said:

1. It was an essential part of good management and good workmanship.
2. Management and workpeople must co-operate to secure freedom from accident.
3. Top management must take the lead in organizing safety in the works.
4. There must be a defined and known safety policy in each workplace.
5. The organization and resources necessary to carry out this policy must exist.
6. The best available knowledge and methods must be used.

Safety committees were to be found in most large and

medium-sized factories, and in some small ones too.* Some were effective, enjoying the continuing interest and enthusiasm of all ranks, others started with a flourish, which lost its momentum before many weeks passed, and the dull apathy of boredom settled on the meetings that were held and the propaganda they put out. It is hard to know how to combat dullness of this kind; it is probably time someone made a survey of successful committees to see why they are so. A quotation from the 1957 report of the chief inspector of factories might fittingly end this section. 'Brief enthusiastic campaigns against accidents have their uses, but it is only through systematic training, and the stimulation of co-operation between workers and management that new habits of safety can be formed among workers, and safety-consciousness encouraged.'

* The industrial accident prevention report (1956) showed that large factories had more joint safety committees than smaller ones. Those employing over 500 had such committees in three out of five cases. Those with 250 to 500 had one committee in every four factories, while those under 250 but with 100 or more employees had only one committee in ten firms, while in the smallest firms the number was negligible. As the accident rate rose with the size of the firm, these figures illustrated the urgency of the problem in the larger factories.

REFERENCES

1. *Railway Labourers*. Select Cttee. Report. p. 427. (1846 (530) xiii.)
2. *The Times*. 18. 11. 1958.
3. Trades Union Congress. Annual Report of General Council, 1959.
4. *International Labour Review*. July 1953.
5. T.U.C. op. cit. 1959.
6. *Industrial Health Services*. Cttee. Report. (1950–51 Cmd. 8170, xv.)
7. 1955 Chief Inspector of Factories Annual Report and 1958 Report on Industrial Health. (1956–7 Cmnd. 8, xii and 1958–9 Cmnd. 811, xiii.)
8. 1957 Industrial Health. Chief Inspector of Factories Annual Report. (1958–9 Cmnd. 558, xiii.)
9. *Rehabilitation of persons injured by accidents*. Inter-dept. Cttee. (Delevingne, Ch.) Reports. 1937, 1939. Non-Parl. Home Office, Min. of Health.
10. *Rehabilitation and Resettlement of disabled persons*. Cttee. (Tomlinson, Ch.) Report. (1942–3 Cmd. 6415, vi.)
11. *Southern Daily Echo*. 25.10.1959.
12. *The Times*. 27.10.1959. Mr. P. Clarkson, Casualty Officer, Guy's Hospital, London.
13. Delevingne Reports 1937, 1939. op. cit. and *Industrial Health Services Report*. op. cit. (1950–51 Cmd. 8170, xv.)
14. *The Times*. 9.11.1959.
15. *The Times*. 26.3.1961.
16. *Industrial Accident Prevention*. National Joint Advisory Council. Industrial Safety Sub-Cttee. Report. 1956 Non-Parl. Min. of Labour.

PART TWO

Statutory System of Cash Benefit for Industrial Injury and Disease

Part II is concerned with an examination of the policy adopted by Great Britain in the provision of cash benefit to injured workers from 1897 onwards; of the way in which the Workmen's Compensation Acts operated, and how, in spite of their manifold advantages, there were too many mistakes for them to be able to continue; of why the growing weight of odium that surrounded them led to demands for change, what the change was, and how the new policy, in some of its details so similar to the old, has created an entirely new situation for the worker injured through his employment.

4

THE WORKMEN'S COMPENSATION ACTS, 1897 ONWARDS

FOR the purposes of this part of the study a distinction will be drawn between employers' liability for accidents that were due to the employers' negligence, the subject of Part III, and the compensation a workman could claim because he had suffered injury. In 'employers' liability' the injured man or his relatives had to prove negligence by the employer. In 'workmen's compensation' the criterion was injury (or disease or death). Thus, though the Employers' Liability Act of 1880 was a forerunner of the Workmen's Compensation Act of 1897, it was based on a different principle, and one much less advantageous to the workman. People grew increasingly discontented with it, and finally found spokesmen in Mr. Asquith and Mr. Joseph Chamberlain to press Parliament for change. An abortive Bill was introduced in 1893, and after the general election of 1895, legislation was assured. Prior to this time there had been two views about what to do. On the one hand, the advocates of prevention wished so to burden the employer with his liability, in cases of accident, that he would have a direct financial incentive to improve the safety of his works and lessen the possible risks. The compensationists, on the other hand, preferred to concentrate on the injured man himself, and assure him of adequate relief when he needed it. The compensationists prevailed, and the legislation veered towards relief of the injured rather than promotion of safety, thus stamping inexorably on the British system the separation between these two aspects.

The main principles of the Act were summed up by Lord Brampton as having[1] 'conferred upon a large class of workmen, whose necessities compelled them to seek employment in certain specified dangerous occupations, in the course of which accidents, not always possible to be guarded against, are of frequent occurrence, some purely casual, others no doubt attributable to negligence or default of fellow workmen, whom it would be idle to sue, or others whose identity could not be established, a right to claim compensation. Such compensation would be to a moderate and limited amount in respect of the loss of such wages as they were incapacitated from earning in consequence of the injury, upon mere proof of the accident and its resulting loss, irrespective of its cause. Another object was to impose the obligation of providing such statutory compensation upon those, to whom good sense would naturally point as the fittest persons to bear it, and to define for the convenience of the injured workmen seeking compensation, the persons from whom they are entitled to claim it. And further to provide a simple proceeding, entailing comparatively trifling expense, by which such compensation might if necessary be enforced'. Thus was a complicated measure simply and optimistically described.

The chief principles of the Act may be reduced to seven, and they deserve examination, because there is hardly one principle that has been wholly free from attack, or which has not added to the mounting discontent that eventually led to complete disruption.

1. The first necessity was to define the scope of industrial injury. This was described, in the now famous phrase, as any personal injury occurring by accident 'arising out of, and in the course of employment'. What is meant by these words has been the source of an infinite variety of litigation. After more than sixty years the meaning is now fairly well understood, though there are still borderline cases about which decisions have to be taken. In the early years of the Act, on the other hand, the difficulties were manifold. Take for instance the case of the boy who broke his arm when he fell off his bicycle. Where and when he fell, and under what circumstances, were crucial to the case, and the giving or withholding of compensation depended on the answer. He

might have fallen on the street on his way to work, or he may have fallen within the factory gates on his arrival; he might have been sent to deliver a message and have fallen in the street, or he might have been playing around the factory grounds in his lunch hour and taken a spill. The many permutations of this theme may be imagined, each of them leading to the same boy breaking his arm and being absent from work, unable to earn his wages, and unable to add his quota to the productivity of the firm. But whether he was eligible for workman's compensation depended on how his case fitted into the phrase 'arising out of *and* in the course of his employment'. In 1897 the phrase 'on, in or about the employer's premises' had also been inserted, but as this was withdrawn in 1906, it was not a major item in the development of the scheme.

2. When once an industrial injury had occurred, the Act established the principle that the employer was liable to pay compensation. There was no longer any necessity to prove the employer guilty of negligence. For in all cases, whether it was his fault or no, he had to pay. The one exception to this was the gross negligence of the injured workman himself. If the employer could prove he had been disobedient to express orders about using safety devices, for instance, the worker would have to bear the consequences, if he was alive to do so. But if he had died as a result of the accident, then no matter how negligent he had been, his dependents could claim compensation from the employer.

It must not be thought that the interpretation of the words 'employer' or 'worker' has been without its difficulties, e.g. workers are lent by one employer to another, contractors let out their work to sub-contractors. A great deal of litigation centred round the exact person upon whom liability rested.

3. The first Act was meant to apply to 'dangerous' trades only, viz., railways, mines, quarries, engineering works, certain building undertakings, and factories, so it was limited in range. By 1900, agriculture was added to the list, but in 1906 the principle was abandoned altogether, being replaced by a more inclusive schedule, depending partly on the income of the worker.

4. The principle of 'contracting out' was allowed on condition the workmen were safeguarded. This principle was no new one, and had been important in the operation of the 1880 Employers' Liability Act. For in 1882, by a judicial finding,[2] it was declared

legal for an employer to make an agreement with his workers to contract out of the scheme. This meant that, when a man took a job, his contract could include an undertaking by him not to claim damages in the event of an accident. Clearly, workers were at a disadvantage if contracting out were widely used, and the emerging trade unions bent much of their energy to have the matter righted. Contracting out in the 1897 Act was therefore tolerated only if the worker was covered by a scheme not less favourable than the new one, and the Registrar of Friendly Societies was appointed to certify that the alternative schemes were as good or better than workmen's compensation itself.

5. Calculation of the compensation was, from the workers' standpoint, the most important part of the Act, and certain principles had to be thought out to govern the situation.

(*a*) The first was, should the employer bear the total liability of an accident and pay compensation equal to a full wage? During the nineteenth century it had been legally argued that when a workman accepted wages and entered a contract of labour, he normally accepted the responsibility for the ordinary risks of his employment (the principle of *volenti non fit injuria*). While there had been some modification of the application of this principle in late nineteenth-century legislation (notably the 1880 Employers' Liability Act), it was not one that could be wholly abandoned by the legislators of 1897. Therefore, it was thought that a worker should share with the employer the consequences of an accident. Moreover, many accidents occurred through circumstances beyond the employers' control, and were frequently aggravated by some negligence on the workers' part. That each should bear an equal share was thought to be a fair and equitable solution of the problem. Thus compensation was fixed at not more than half a man's annual average wage. This principle remained with certain modifications until the scheme was abandoned. Yet, almost from its inception, it was attacked as mean, and a hardship to an injured man and his family. No other modern industrialized state tolerated so low a percentage (most others paid compensation up to two-thirds of the wage). But in spite of strong representations, particularly from the Holman Gregory Committee in 1920, little was done to alter the proportion.

(*b*) The exact meaning of an annual average wage had to be found, and a great many court decisions were sought about overtime pay, what should happen if a man had changed his employer within the year, whether a 'normal' wage was an 'average' wage, the effect of periods of inflation. All these questions, and many more, kept the lawyers busy and the injured workman on tenterhooks over the years.

(*c*) A statutory limitation to the wage percentage concept was written into the earliest Workmen's Compensation Act, in the principle of the maximum. For, in order that employers should be safeguarded against unlimited claims, it was laid down that the compensation should not exceed £1 a week. In 1897 this was not ungenerous, since a skilled workman would earn up to £2 per week. Nor was the burden on industry likely to be onerous, as these limitations ensured that payment for injury would not materially affect prices. Thus the Holman Gregory Committee was able to report in 1920,[3] that in the majority of industries, the cost represented only a fraction of a penny in the £1 on the price of an article; while even in coal mining, the most hazardous of all industries, the cost added only twopence to the price of each ton. But it was a principle that was severely challenged throughout the history of the Acts.

(*d*) A variant of the weekly payment was the 'lump sum', by which the employer or the worker could agree to forego all rights to weekly payment, in return for a down-payment of a sum of money. A worker and his employer could at any time agree to this method, and the employer (not the worker) had the right, after six months of weekly payments, to redeem his obligation by a lump sum if he wished. Most injuries, which had lasted more than six months, would be likely to be permanent, and in that case the lump sum was to be thought of as an annuity, and was to be registered at the County Court, with the County Court Judge acting as a referee on the amount. This kind of payment had certain advantages, as it gave the injured man a capital sum with which to meet outstanding debts, or pay for new equipment, or start a business. It ended any worry he might have endured about the continuation of his benefit, and it was alleged many men found themselves a job within their capacity when they were assured that their benefit was no longer endangered by such an action. The employer also benefited by limiting his future expenditure and making a fair allotment to his employee. Lump sums were not always as straightforward as this, because they were sometimes paid instead of a weekly sum, where the employer disputed his liability but was willing to give the man money to close the incident. Such payments, being made by agreement between the parties, were not registered at the court, and were therefore not supervised, as to amount, by any official or experienced person. No other industrial country up to 1939 adopted the 'lump sum' method.

(*e*) A further important matter was the problem of when an accident would count as a compensation case. If a man was slightly hurt and was absent a day or two should he receive benefit? If this were so, it was argued, the expense to the employer would be very great and quite out of proportion to what might fairly be thought of as an employer's liability. A minimum period of three weeks was at first fixed as the criterion; and though later this was reduced to two weeks, the principle of the waiting period (after 1948 reduced to three days) continued.

(*f*) Injury and incapacity are one thing, death is another. For now it was not the injured person who shared the cost of his injury with the employer, but his dependents. Up to this point, the whole tone of the Act had been to create a partnership in adversity between the employer and his injured worker, but the latter's death raised humanitarian considerations about his domestic responsibilities. Nevertheless the principle of payment according to the man's average wage persisted even here, and in the early years of the Act no account was taken of his children, only of his widow (or other dependent – like mother, sister, father) to whom a lump sum not exceeding £300 was paid, according to the wages he had earned, the length of time he had been in the one employment, and the degree of the dependence.

6. No complicated measure of this kind could hope to function without dispute. It had been the original aim of the measure not to depend on the courts for its operation, but to create a system in which a man injured at work could simply and quickly receive benefit from his employer. In the majority of cases this spirit prevailed; and everyone hoped that, if disputes arose, they could be settled by friendly negotiation or by some tribunal helping to solve the problem with the least fuss and expenditure. Only in exceptional cases was it thought likely that the matter would have to be taken to court. On looking back it is hard to understand this optimism. For when a large number of individuals are poten-

tial beneficiaries, and another large number of individuals are liable to pay unforeseeable amounts of money out of their own pockets, it stands to reason that a litigious situation is created. The recourse to insurance, and the impersonal factors thus introduced, far from reducing the incidence of court action, would be likely to increase it, since any decision became a precedent for subsequent action. However, the 1897 Act made it possible for most compensation cases to be settled out of court, whereas before then, few could be.

7. Because the whole burden of the cost of workmen's compensation was thrown on the employer, it followed that the burden varied according to the risk. This was defended by the Home Secretary, when the Bill was introduced, on the grounds that[4] 'when a person on his own responsibility and for his own profit sets in motion agencies which create risks for others, he ought to be responsible for what he does'. Thus an employer who insured against his statutory liability could expect to pay premiums according to the risks of his business, and the man who did not insure would have to pay according to the accidents that occurred. In the more dangerous industries the costs were high. As most employers insured, it would have seemed logical for the variations in premiums to provide an incentive to develop safety measures. But apparently the variations were not great enough, so the system did not have the expected effect.

After 1897

The fifty years of the Workmen's Compensation Acts were full of committees of inquiry, of discontent and agitation for change, of charges of malingering, and counter-charges that certain employers were evading their responsibility (e.g. by going into bankruptcy), of schemes for reform, of the building up of a welter of case law, and of a few modifications in the scheme itself. But in spite of a half century of social and economic change, such as the world had never before witnessed, the main outlines of the workmen's compensation scheme remained intact.

Yet changes there were during these years, changes that require examination, not because of the improvements they brought, great though these were, but because of the public concern that gave rise to them, and the subsequent events that were shaped by them.

1. *Coverage of personnel*

The 1897 Act had been deliberately selective, and confined to workers employed in dangerous industries. Yet as early as 1904 a committee of inquiry was advocating a break in this principle, and the substitution of an inclusive coverage. Thus, in the Workmen's Compensation Act of 1906, an employer's liability to compensate an injured workman was extended to all manual workers, and non-manual workers if they earned under £250 a year. Certain exceptions to this rule were named, e.g. casual workers, outworkers, the police and members of an employer's family living with him. This was five years before the passing of the National [Health] Insurance Act, highly selective in its early stages, though after World War I the most comprehensive of all the national insurance schemes. Yet even this scheme was not more comprehensive than workmen's compensation had been in 1906. The Unemployment Insurance Acts remained selective until they were superseded by the great changes of 1946–8. That industrial injury compensation should have been available on such a wide basis, from such an early date, is a remarkable feature of British social legislation. Accordingly, its extension to all persons under contract of service in 1946 was not the revolutionary step that similar extensions were in the other 'national insurances' (particularly in the case of retirement benefit).

2. *Family Allowances*

We have seen how, in ordinary cases of injury, a man could expect to receive a weekly sum in proportion to his normal average wage, subject to a maximum, but that in the case of his death, his dependents were compensated, also in proportion to the wage he earned, and the length of service. No mention was made in either case of his children. This was deliberate policy and was supported as late as 1920 by the Holman Gregory Committee who argued that as wages did not vary according to a worker's needs, neither should injury compensation. A worker's domestic affairs, they said, were no concern of the employer, and were they to become so might severely embarrass the worker. However they were prepared to concede that in a fatal accident a man's family should be considered. The practice up to the end of the First World War in the case of death had been to pay a lump sum into a court, by whom the money was invested, and paid out at intervals until it was exhausted. All agreed that the fund was frequently exhausted long before the family had ceased to need its help. Further, they agreed that as no account was taken of the size of the family, the age of the children and their length of dependency, much unfairness resulted. For instance an elderly widow with no children could receive as much as, and probably more than, a young widow with a large number of little children. They therefore recommended that where death resulted from an accident two kinds of payment should be made – the first a lump sum for the widow, and the second a weekly payment for each child until he reached the age of fifteen. They were prepared to establish a maintenance grant for a child even though he might have left school at fourteen and started work. In 1923 new legislation was introduced to enable some of the Holman Gregory recommendations to operate. Though it did not go as far as the committee wished, it did for the first time introduce the element of need into workmen's compensation by enacting that in the event of death, the widow should receive a lump sum (maximum £200) and that a further lump sum not exceeding £600 should be paid in respect of the children, having regard to their number and age. Both sums would normally be paid into the County Court, and dispensed in weekly amounts. But of family allowances as part of compensation for an injured man there was no mention. Yet the principle had been accepted elsewhere. For under the Unemployment Insurance Acts, a wife and children did receive benefit if the husband were unemployed. In national health insurance, on the other hand, dependents were excluded from benefit and as this was closer to workers' compensation than unemployment insurance, the anomaly continued. World War II was to bring a change. The campaign for family allowances for all was gaining momentum; there was also a growing repugnance to the fact that a sick or injured man should have to seek supplementation of his benefit from the Poor Law. At last, in 1940, family allowances for men on workmen's compensation were introduced. Admittedly these children's allowances were hedged round with provisos, such as the requirement that total benefit should not exceed seven-eighths of the pre-accident wage. But the principle was accepted, and the way was clear for the future.

3. *Diseases*

It was strange that industrial diseases were not included in the original Act, because in 1833 a Factories Inquiry Commission had shown the connexion between conditions in factories and certain diseases, and in 1879 the chief inspector of factories had included a section in his annual report entitled 'occupations injurious to health'. It was not until the Workmen's Compensation Act of 1906 that certain diseases 'due to the nature of the employment' carried compensation. The schedule of diseases has been reviewed and lengthened as the years have passed, and the principle of associating the disease with certain risky industries and of requiring the sufferers to have been a minimum time at risk, has continued. Efforts have been made from time to time to allow anyone suffering from the specified disease to receive benefit, whether he has worked in the stated industry or not. But these efforts have been firmly resisted.

The onset of disease is a medical matter, and this has had most interesting practical results. For the profession of medicine, being concerned with prevention as well as cure, has stimulated industrial doctors (and others) to busy themselves from early times with research into the causes of industrial disease, as well as the best methods of treating and curing the patients. Medical efforts of this kind have reached vast proportions (e.g. the study of pneumoconiosis by the National Coal Board) and all branches of industry have worked together to achieve an outstanding improvement in the incidence of industrial diseases among workers. Thus, whereas workmen's compensation for accident did not lead directly to research and improvement, compensation for disease has focused attention upon an amelioration of the position.

4. *Insurance*

As might have been anticipated when the first Act was passed, most employers insured against the risk of compensation to their workers. One result of this was that the insurance companies found themselves with a large and growing side to their business, which had to be changed and modified as knowledge accumulated. Out of this rose the suggestion that employers should be compelled to insure, so that the rights of injured workmen would be safeguarded; and further, that as insurance was so necessary and relatively universal, it ought to be taken out of private hands and transferred to the state. The seeds of the present system were therefore inherent in the situation as it developed after 1897, and some analysis of the insurance companies' contribution to workmen's compensation is appropriate.

Within the first decade of the establishment of compulsory compensation, the government introduced a measure to ensure that insurance companies would not be of straw, but could meet any sudden and large demands made on them.

In 1907 an Employers' Liability Insurance Companies Act was passed, later to be incorporated in the Assurance Companies Act of 1909. Each company undertaking this kind of business was obliged to deposit £20,000 with the Board of Trade (unless the company had transacted such business before 28 August, 1907). It must also keep separate funds for its business carried on under the headings of Life, Industrial, Employers' Liability, and Bond Investment Insurance, though its investments need not be separated. The £20,000 deposit was not intended as a reserve in times of difficulty, though it sometimes did act in that way, but as an earnest of the financial stability of the company. Further, each company was obliged to make annual returns to the Board of Trade, giving details of the business, outstanding claims, etc. These could be published and became increasingly important as a source of information about the working of the Compensation Acts. The Board did not appoint inspectors, nor were they concerned to see that a company remained solvent, though, by later Acts (Assurance Companies (Winding Up) Acts 1933 and 1935), they could send in inspectors if they had reason to think a company might be going bankrupt; but the government maintained some control so that the money would be there when it was needed. On the other hand, there was nothing in the Acts to give the government the right to interfere in how the companies carried on their business which, like any other private enterprise, was conducted on a competitive basis, and brought a profit to the shareholders.

The 1909 Act has been amended several times but not repealed. However, in 1946 it was decided to abolish the deposit system, because the National Insurance Acts had made it unnecessary as a safeguard for the worker, and modern conditions had made it out of date. Insurance companies, by this time, were international in their business, and as many countries had followed the example of Britain in demanding a £20,000 deposit, companies found themselves with comparable sums deposited in each of a number of countries, and capital that might have been profitably invested was lying idle. Further, £20,000 was of little value as a measure of a company's standing under modern monetary values.

Though the profit motive was undoubtedly uppermost in company policy, there was some flexibility in their interpretation of legislation. For instance, in 1919 an Act was passed giving the Home Office the right to relieve an employer in whole, or in part, of any losses he might sustain in employing a disabled man (usually this meant a war victim). The insurance companies, in their turn, agreed not to charge higher premiums for the insurance of the disabled. They covered themselves by keeping separate accounts, so that if the disabled became an unduly heavy charge, the Home Office might come to their rescue. The Act itself was terminated in 1921, but insurers continued to declare on their forms that no higher premiums would be charged to employers in respect of disabled soldiers, sailors and airmen.

Again, in 1923, after the publication of the Holman Gregory Report which had recommended a certain amount of compulsory insurance for workmen's compensation purposes and state supervision of the company's profits and expenses on this branch of their work, the companies made an offer. They did this to forestall government control, and the fact that they did it voluntarily was an indication of their awareness of public opinion and, they claimed, of concern for public need. The offer was made by the Accident Offices Association, and was drawn up on 24 May, 1923 (Cmd. 1891) and is generally known as the 'Home Office Agreement'. The Association, on behalf of its members, agreed to adjust the rates of premium so that the loss ratio (i.e. payment of claims) was not less than an agreed percentage. Should the 'loss ratio' fall short of this, the companies would allow the policy-holders a 'special rebate'. In this way, the companies voluntarily limited their profits and expenses to the 30 per cent of premium which the Holman Gregory Committee had thought sufficient, and passed on the benefit to the policy-holders. The average rebate each year, during the currency of the Agreement (1924–46), was just over 7 per cent. The non-tariff insurers were also consulted, and agreed to work a system that was said to be a 'more economic arrangement than is to be found in the working of insurance companies in any other country'.[5]

These instances have been quoted, because subsequently the insurance companies were said to have used a disproportionate amount of premium in expenses and profits, allowing too small an allocation for the payment of claims. This may well have been so, but the companies were not unaware of the criticism, or unwilling to remedy the position by any methods that were open to them, while still having regard to the interests of the shareholders.

A further aspect of the financing of workmen's compensation claims was the establishment of mutual indemnity associations by groups of employers for the purpose. The difference between these and insurance companies was that, while the latter charged premiums to cover all eventualities, and made them high enough to meet costs, reserves and profits as well, the mutual indemnities charged no premium at all, need have no profits and no reserves, but could call upon the members periodically to pay the claims in an agreed proportion. In practice the mutual indemnity associations were not quite so haphazard as this. A few were hardly distinguishable from ordinary insurance companies. But most held small reserves with little margin in the event of a large call upon funds. This was of small moment so long as member firms were prosperous. But in times of bad trade, not uncommon in the inter-war period, the weaknesses of the situation became apparent.

In 1936 the Board of Trade set up a committee[6] (Cassel Committee) to look into the whole question, particularly as it referred to coal mining, because more than 70 per cent of the colliery companies had joined one or other of the mutual indemnity associations. Compensation claims were very high in coal mining, e.g. in 1934 two and a half million pounds had been paid out in respect of nearly 175,000 claimants. Further, it was hard to tell what the future liabilities of workmen's compensation would be. This was true of all industries, but was worse in coal mining because of the nature of the work and the troubles it gave rise to. 'Catastrophe' risks were all too common and, while some mutuals re-insured with Lloyds (e.g. the Gresham disaster was so covered), others did not, and a disaster of any magnitude could bring the member firms to bankruptcy. 'Latent liability' was another risk. Pneumoconiosis, for instance, could reappear, and the employer might find himself liable years afterwards.

It was the Cassel Committee's view that there was not enough control over these mutual associations, and the danger that a workman might find himself without compensation due to their default was a real one. They recommended that, as solvency was the most important criterion, mutual indemnity associations, and any other private compensation trusts, should submit to the Assurance Companies Acts 1909–1935, and should be obliged to publish information about themselves. (The Cassel Committee had the utmost difficulty in obtaining information and was only given confidential reports on condition that nothing would be published that could identify the association.) They should also deposit £20,000 with the Board of Trade, and allow inspectors access if there was any danger of bankruptcy. Moreover, the associations should act on strict insurance principles, and levy premiums for a stated period of not more than twelve months during which a member would be covered. They should make the premiums high enough to meet the capitalized value of claims arising during the period; and 'catastrophe' risks should be re-insured. The committee thought that more co-operation and supervision was required, and suggested the establishment of three advisory committees at the Board of Trade, concerned respectively with insurance companies, mutual indemnity associations, and Lloyd's. The Second World War prevented the implementation of these proposals, and in any case, a Royal Commission to consider afresh the whole question of workers' compensation, was appointed in 1938 under Sir Hector Hetherington.*

Meanwhile there remained the question of whether employers should be compelled to insure and, if so, the much larger one, of whether the State should be the insurer. It is understandable that, from its earliest years, the system of workmen's compensation bred speculation and discussion about finance. A departmental committee report in 1907 (Farrer Report) discussed whether employers should be compelled to insure, but decided against, on the grounds that it was unworkable. Thirteen years later, the Holman Gregory Committee thought it was feasible, and recommended compulsory insurance with private insurance companies

* It suspended sittings in 1940. Its work was taken up by Sir W. Beveridge.

against compensation claims in much the same way as third party risks in motoring were to be insured later. Nothing was done about this, except in the case of coal mining, where, after a severe catastrophe, followed by bankruptcy, injured miners found themselves without any compensation. In 1934, the Nicholson Act was passed in an attempt to prevent such a situation happening again. It was not very satisfactory, as it was limited to colliery owners, and the principle of compulsory insurance applied only to accidents and diseases that had lasted more than six months. So, apart from this halting beginning nothing was done; though the Cassel Committee, reporting three years later, again recommended that insurance should be compulsory and should cover the whole period, including the first twenty-six weeks. For, they said, though there might be advantages in retaining a completely free and fluid relationship between worker and master in the short-run, because re-employment in the old job or in a more suitable one in the firm could be encouraged, the dangers outweighed these; and, in any case, compulsory insurance would not of itself break the tie between employer and worker.

There were other grievances brewing up besides possible loss of compensation through the bankruptcy of the employer. Because these were so many, and the climate of the times was changing so rapidly, the problem of a compulsory state-run insurance was shelved. What these grievances were, and how they led to a new blue-print for benefit in cases of industrial injury, is the subject of the next chapter.

REFERENCES

1. A. Wilson & H. Levy, *Workmen's Compensation.* (Oxford U.P. 1939.) Vol. I. p. 63.
2. *Griffiths vs. Earl of Dudley.* [1882.] 9 Q.B.D. 357.
3. *Workmen's Compensation.* Cttee. (Holman Gregory. Ch.) Rep. p. 42. (1920 Cmd. 816, xxvi.)
4. *Social Insurance and Allied Services.* Cttee. (Beveridge, Ch.) Report. p. 41. (1942–3 Cmd. 6404, vi.)
5. W. A. Dinsdale, *History of Accident Insurance.* (Buckley, 1956.) p. 159.
6. *Compulsory Insurance.* Board of Trade Cttee. (Cassel, Ch.) Report. (1936–7 Cmd. 5528, xii.)

5

WEAKNESSES OF WORKMEN'S COMPENSATION

COMPLAINTS about the working of the workmen's compensation scheme did not come, in the main, from the employers upon whom the direct burden lay, but from the injured workers and their trade unions. Accordingly this section will be divided into two parts: grievances by employees, and general criticisms.

I. *Workers' grievances*

As one would expect, these centred round the amount of cash benefit they received, and their difficulties in establishing their claims.

(*a*) *Weekly payment*

Because weekly compensation was based on the man's average wage, subject to a maximum, there was a strong feeling of injustice on how this was calculated. The average wage over the previous year might have been less than the normal, through no fault of the worker. He might have been held up through scarcity of material, or through working a bad seam (as in coal), or through bad weather (as in building). Moreover, in times of inflation, he might find himself on a compensation calculated according to a lower general level of wages, while obliged to meet costs of living that were rising. Several adjustments of the maximum during the years made some allowance for this, but not enough. The general principle of compensation had been to take no account of need, but to offer a percentage of past income. This principle was early breached in the case of death, but it was not until 1940 that children's allowances were added to the ordinary weekly payments of an injured man. Even the percentage of income was a bone of contention. For, though 50 per cent had been originally agreed upon as a fair allocation of responsibility between employer and employee, times had changed, and in any case it was a poor figure compared with other countries. In 1920 the Holman Gregory Committee had reported on the higher rates paid elsewhere and, in subsequent years, at committees of inquiry, and through the International Labour Office (1939), attempts were made to raise the proportion to two-thirds. Apart from a few cases of very poorly paid workers (1923), or young workers, the 50 per cent ratio remained until 1940, when it was more seriously assailed in the case of married men with children, who might be allowed to receive up to seven-eighths of their former wage. This reform, valuable though it was, could not save the system of workmen's compensation, as the mischief had been done.

(b) Lump Sum

Unpopular as was the rate of weekly compensation, it seems to have been less subject to abuse than the 'lump sum in lieu'. As we have seen, it was possible for both parties to agree on commuting the compensation at any time, and for the employer to do so after six months, provided the matter was registered with the County Court. Opposition to the idea, according to Beveridge, arose either because the sum offered was not enough, or because it was injudiciously expended, or because it encouraged a man to make the most of his injury and delay recovery in the hope of obtaining a larger sum. These objections had been voiced to the Holman Gregory Committee,[2] to whom the Ministry of Pensions had declared that in their experience the device of the lump sum was 'on the whole not successful'. However the committee was not minded to forbid it, though they recommended a tightening-up of the administration, especially the proper registration with the court. They wanted to see the attendance of both parties, if there was a hearing, with the provision of adequate medical reports, and reference to a medical referee in cases of dispute. These recommendations were enacted later. One proposal the committee did not approve was that the worker should have the same right as the employer to demand a lump sum after six months. The trade unions had asked for it on grounds of equity, and also because in many cases their members preferred the money in their hands, rather than a weekly dole that might stretch out endlessly. But the Holman Gregory Committee opposed it, because since it was the employers who had to pay, it ought to rest with them how the payment should be made. Moreover, should an employer be faced with a number of demands for commutation, he might be grievously embarrassed. And so the matter stood.

Before the scheme was finally altered there appeared a pair of redoubtable opponents to attack the 'lump sum' in Sir Arnold Wilson and Professor Levy, who published their study of 'Workmen's Compensation' in 1939.[3] They could see no good in the 'lump sum' at all and their examination of the facts, and the arguments they used, certainly added up to a powerful indictment. Take for instance the argument of popularity. The lump sum was said to be popular with the worker, because it provided him with some capital to buy a house or a business. Yet in practice this seldom followed. More often he used the money to pay off his debts, or to live at a higher standard for a few months, only to find, when the money was gone, that his disability remained and he had no means of livelihood. The Ministry of Pensions, they said, had used the device sparingly, and only when they were assured that the money would be put into a house, a business or used for emigrating. All applications for the commuting of a war pension had been closely examined and, should a pensioner apply to start a business, he was required to state the nature of the business, his own experience and skill, whether he meant to buy a going concern, or start *de novo*. Refusals were more common than acceptances. Of nearly 45,000 applications for lump sum settlement between 1921–38, only 2,500 were accepted, fewer than 6 per cent. Even so, when in 1935 Professor Levy made a test inquiry into fifty-eight businesses started by means of these Ministry of Pensions lump sum payments in 1928 and 1929, twenty-five pensioners only were found to be still in business. Of the others, twenty-three suffered total or partial loss and had given up, and the other ten could not be traced. So in spite of the Ministry's safeguards, there were probably more failures than successes. As no such safeguards were demanded in workmen's compensation, the value of the lump sum as a means of earning a livelihood, and thus a permanent compensation for injury, became very doubtful.

It was said also to be popular with the employers. But it was Levy's opinion that employers welcomed it as a means of quickly getting rid of an obligation on the most advantageous terms. Bargaining was, in most cases, integral to the lump sum process and, in bargaining, the employer (or more often the insurance company) was the stronger party. If it remained a private agreement, in which the injured man argued his own case, he was nearly always at a disadvantage in face of the far more experienced insurance assessor. If it went to court the same was true. The worker's legal and medical advice, fortuitously secured, must almost always be inferior to the insurance company's standing counsel, regular solicitor, and salaried medical adviser. A system so heavily weighted might well be popular with the employers, yet fail to do justice to the injured man and his family, and the future prospects and security of his life.

The very fact that lump sum settlements so frequently involved protracted negotiations was another objection to the whole device. During the negotiations the injured man was worried and frustrated by the delay, and his physical condition could deteriorate, while his mental state might also suffer setback. 'Lump sum neurosis' was well known, and could be perverted into 'malingering' to obtain a lump sum, or be simply an anxiety state arising out of the delay and uncertainty. In either case the result was contrary to the best interests both of the man and his productive potential.

Levy was suspicious of the administrative proceedings too. The system of vetting all compensation agreements by the court registrar was not as carefully operated as it should have been, and where the matter came before the court the judge seldom questioned the decisions arrived at. Furthermore a different court might bring a different decision, and so a man's future was uncertain, and liable to be influenced by incidental factors.

Objections so widely held, and in Wilson and Levy's book so robustly stated, had built such a formidable case against the 'lump sum' system, that it is surprising the government decided to retain it when the new legislation was drafted.

(*c*) *Review of Case*

From the early days of the Act, injured workmen complained about the hostility they met when seeking to improve their compensation, or to resist the employer's demands for its reduction or withdrawal. Three sets of medical opinion could be involved: the man's own doctor, a doctor selected or appointed (sometimes employed full-time by insurance companies) by the employer, and the medical referee (part-time) appointed by the court. The injured man could seldom afford more than his own panel doctor, and only if he was supported by a wealthy trade union could he call on the services of a consultant to speak for him in court. Insurance companies, on the other hand, usually employed several full-time medical consultants, and had the funds to call in others when necessary. The courts relied, in the main, on general practitioners (part-time), whose functions were threefold:[4] (*a*) to testify to the registrar on the physical condition of an injured man if there was a joint request for revision of compensation from both employer and worker; (*b*) to sit in the court with the judge as an assessor, i.e. to advise the judge what 'inferences may properly be drawn on the medical issues from the facts presented in evidence'. The judge had to decide the case and was free to accept or reject the medical advice so given, but he would reject it only on the most compelling grounds; (*c*) at the request of the judge, arbitrator, or committee, to report on any material matter arising in arbitration.

It was therefore possible for a man to be examined by two sets of medical personnel, as well as his own doctor, and it was because of the alleged hostility he had to face from the outside experts that so much discontent arose. Accusations of this kind are difficult to prove, but the fact they were so widespread tended to give the whole system a bad name, and increased the growing clamour for its reorganization. It cannot be denied that in very many cases of dispute over an injured man's condition, the man felt himself to be, and was, at a disadvantage when faced with the opinions of highly placed medical men. It was useless for him to argue that his own doctor, who saw him regularly, was more likely to know his true condition, than the medical referees who saw him at the examination only.

(d) Disputes

The other aspect of the workers' dissatisfaction with the whole system of compensation was the difficulty they so often experienced in establishing their claims at all. In spite of the original intentions of the 1897 Act, each year it operated saw a large number of court cases to decide the issues that arose. Sir Matthew White Ridley, then Home Secretary, was woefully wrong when he declared during the Bill's debate in 1897 that it[5] 'is defined and limited, so that both parties may know where they stand; it provides an inexpensive method of settling questions that must arise, and if it be true that legislation of this kind ought to aim at being simple, immediate and effective, this Bill has been conceived with that object'. From the very beginning, complaints were made about the way injured men had to fight for their compensation; how they were questioned as they lay in hospital, how their recovery was retarded by the anxiety they felt, and how the worry of an impending court case, and the fear that it would go against them, added to the pain and suffering of the illness itself. Even in 1904 the departmental committee to consider the working of the Compensation Act discussed the matter, though their conclusion was that the number of court cases was remarkably small, when the complexity of the Act was considered, and was small compared with the number settled otherwise. It was not necessary to take every dispute to the County Court (or failing that, the High Court). Single arbitrators could be appointed. In practice this hardly ever happened, and, though the Cumberland and Durham Miners had set up joint arbitration committees which were reasonably successful, these were the only examples of voluntary standing committees. The usual method was the County Court. The Holman Gregory Committee in 1920[6] claimed there was no evidence of dissatisfaction with this method, though they admitted that different judges came to different decisions on the same facts, and as there were fifty-six County Court judges and 474 registrars, varieties in verdict were infinite. They would like to have recommended the appointment of district commissioners, under a commissioner, to advise and conciliate between the parties and, if necessary, arbitrate in disputes with less formality, delay and expense, than in a court of law. They did not do so because there was no pressure for change, and post-war conditions would have made it difficult. However, they did suggest that judges and registrars should meet frequently to discuss the administration of the Act, and try to achieve more uniformity. They were also ready to agree that an injured man and his family were in a position of weakness in the court, since there was no means of obtaining legal advice, except through the trade union. They would have liked to see the registrars setting themselves up as free legal advice agencies, as they were convinced a little skilled help of this kind would actually prevent a large number of court cases.

The position did not improve with the years. Instead, the feelings of injustice and resentment grew, until by the time the Beveridge Report was issued in 1942, this aspect had begun to assume a predominant position in the list of objections to the scheme. As Beveridge pointed out,[7] all tricky cases had to be settled by litigation, or the threat of it. Such cases might not even be concerned with the man's injury, but with such problems as demarcation between different authorities with different funds. Industrial disease was another complicated matter; the onset could be slow, workmen could have had several employers, and it was often hard to decide in whose employment the disease had begun. There was always the danger that a man showing early signs of a disease might be discharged from his job altogether.

This continuing recourse to law put an intolerable financial burden on the individual, exceeding that of any other form of social security in Great Britain, or of industrial compensation abroad. At no time in the history of trade unionism have any but a minority of the workers belonged, consequently the majority of injured workers have had to face the expense of litigation alone. In fact, said Beveridge, workers' compensation 'has been based on a wrong principle, and has been dominated by a wrong outlook . . . It allows claims to be settled by bargaining between unequal parties, permits payment of socially wasteful sums instead of pensions in cases of serious incapacity; places the cost of medical care on the workman, or charity, or poor relief'.

These sentiments were endorsed by the government when, in 1944, they issued the White Paper. They quite agreed with Beveridge that the scheme was too complicated, and that there was too much scope for contention. They added that this tended to retard a worker's recovery and endangered good relations between employers and employees. Twenty years after the

Holman Gregory Report the government now viewed the large number of court cases with concern. For, though the number was small in proportion to the total decisions made, it amounted to many thousands, and payments, especially lump sum payments, were delayed accordingly. Moreover the injustice of allowing the injured man to fight on an unequal footing was something no longer to be tolerated. Some evidence of the number of cases taken to court was given during the debates on the Industrial Injuries Bill. The Minister of National Insurance stated that 3,000 reported leading cases had been noted, and these were only a fraction of the total number, e.g. in 1938 there were 4,572 applications for arbitration, over half being settled or withdrawn without being heard; in addition 22,454 memoranda were registered, of which 3,136 were for lump sum settlements; and seventy-five appeals had gone to the Court of Appeal.[8]

II. *General Criticisms*

In spite of the fact that the full burden of compensation was borne by the employers, unlike the other facets of the social security system, there appears to have been little complaint from them about its general principles or administration, except perhaps for a somewhat undefined fear that it led to 'malingering'.

(*a*) *Malingering*[9]

The whole question of 'malingering' was investigated by the Holman Gregory Committee in 1920, and while no exact definition was given to the word, it was understood to mean that a man pretended to be ill when he was not, or tended to prolong his illness past the time when he could have been expected to return to work. It was not anything that could be proved, as no doctor could say a man had no pain if he declared he had. But there was a general impression among some employers (though not the workers' representatives who gave evidence) that 'malingering' existed, and was encouraged by the payment of weekly compensation, and even more by the hope of a lump sum. Some said that if an injured worker got benefit through his club as well as from his employer, he might be better off disabled than at work. Others said that the longer a man was away from work, the less inclined he was to return because the habit of work had gone, and inertia had taken its place. They wanted, therefore, a weekly review of payments to be undertaken by the court. One aspect of the administration of compensation in the early days, said to promote 'malingering', was the 'waiting period'. At first no money was paid until after the third week of illness, later it was reduced to two weeks. This had the effect of encouraging men to absent themselves for the minimum number of weeks in order to get the compensation. The Holman Gregory Report quoted comparative figures for the Durham coalfield. In 1906 and 1918 the number of accidents was about the same (17,000) but, whereas in 1906, before the waiting period had been introduced, fewer than half caused absences of as long as two weeks, in 1918, 90 per cent did so. There was general agreement on the committee in favour of three waiting days, to bring workmen's compensation in line with unemployment and health insurance, and this was later adopted. So the 'waiting period' as a source of 'malingering' was ended. Even so, the suspicion about malingering continued, though unsupported by the Holman Gregory Committee, who declared themselves 'satisfied after careful inquiries from employers and insurance company officials, that the average worker wants to return to work as soon as he is able'. Their only rider to this general conclusion was that some workers, suffering from neurosis, did present evidence that looked uncommonly like an attempt to deceive, but that they were few in number. It would be wrong to say that the suspicion has disappeared, but the word 'malingering' is seldom used today, even though the condition is said to be present. However, the blame is not laid at the door of the Workmen's Compensation Acts or their successors, but rather at the more ambiguous entity 'the Welfare State'.

(b) Costs of Compensation

A weakness of the scheme that was laid bare on at least two important occasions by impartial government committees, which paradoxically seemed to attract little displeasure from employers, was the question of value for money by the insurance method. This lack of interest was probably due to the fact that insurance premiums against the risk of compensation were only a small annual expenditure for the employers, and, if they were too high compared with the costs of the national insurances, that was a general criticism, and not one that any employer felt disposed to fight.

However the Holman Gregory Committee were quite outspoken in their concern.[10] For in the period 1911 to 1918 the average annual proportion of insurance companies' expenses was as follows: comisssion 12·1 per cent, expenses of management 19·0 per cent, payments under policies, etc., 51·7 per cent, profits 15·2 per cent, transfers to additional reserves 2·0 per cent. Or to put it another way, for every incoming £1 in the eight-year average, 'not more than 10s. 4d. was spent in payments under policies, 2s. 5d. went in commission, 3s. 10d. in expenses of management, 3s. were disbursed as profit, and 5d. was devoted to transfers to additional reserves'. To the committee this situation was wasteful and unsatisfactory.

When Beveridge[11] came to review the matter he found that the proportions were very little better. In spite of the voluntary effort by the tariff companies to improve the ratio after 1922, and to limit expenses and profits to 30 per cent (which was the Holman Gregory recommendation) so that not less than 70 per cent would be available to pay out in claims, the position had deteriorated. By the late thirties the administrative costs were a full 50 per cent higher than was advocated. Beveridge commented on this, and described the three ways by which employers were wont to meet their liabilities, viz. through the commercial companies, the mutual insurance associations, and the self-insurance schemes. The administrative costs varied greatly between these three methods, for in the years 1938–9 the average percentage spent on them was 46·5 per cent by the commercial companies, 21·6 per cent by the mutual insurance associations, and 10 per cent by the self-insurers. The average he reckoned to be about 19 per cent, which seemed to him unaccountably high – higher than the administrative costs of the national insurances. Though some[12] have claimed that Beveridge did not blame the insurance companies, or reflect on their efficiency, but blamed the system with which they had to deal, Beveridge himself agreed with the Holman Gregory Committee, that a system that did not involve the expense of a weekly visit by an insurance officer to collect the premium (as was common in the 'Life' and other sections of insurance business), was being run at intolerable expense and needed altering.

(c) Rehabilitation and Resettlement

The other general criticism was the absence of any serious effort by those responsible for compensation to promote a co-ordinated scheme of rehabilitation and resettlement. According to Beveridge,[13] the Accident Offices Association, giving evidence before the Royal Commission on workmen's compensation in 1940, described rehabilitation as not being their concern. When the Beveridge Committee took over the work of the Royal Commission during the war, the question was again asked of the accident officers, and a much modified attitude was taken. However, the fact remained that neither the national health insurance (administered by the insurance companies) nor the workers' compensation section concerned themselves to any extent with the well-being of the injured man and his restoration to full working capacity. In this Britain lagged behind other countries. For the U.S.A., Germany and France had had an integrated scheme of rehabilitation as part of their workers' compensation for many years. In spite of successive reports, nothing was done in the United Kingdom except by voluntary organizations such as Lord Roberts Workshops, and the semi-statutory Miners' Welfare Fund.

Closely allied to rehabilitation is resettlement in industry, and here again there was a good deal of general criticism. The original aim of workmen's compensation had been to keep the personal link between the employer and employee so that, in the event of an injury, the injured man could be re-employed in his old job when he was fit enough, or found other work in the firm more suitable to his capacities if he were disabled. There is no doubt that in the majority of cases this is precisely what happened; but there was a large enough minority to create a problem. If the case had gone to litigation, with its inevitable tension and bad feeling, neither the employer nor the man might wish to continue the relationship; and what employment the man then obtained was left to chance. Or it might be that a man was 'signed off' and declared fit for 'light work'. This meant his compensation ended, but not that a job of the 'light' variety was found. Indeed, this matter was discussed at length by the Holman Gregory Committee to whom several witnesses (including some of the County Court judges themselves) complained that 'light work' was not found easily, and that the term was merely a euphemism for ending compensation.

One side of the problem was re-training, and Sir James Currie, from the Ministry of Labour, thought that the scheme already in operation for training war-disabled men, might be extended to civilians injured in industry (i.e. training in a skill in a government training centre for six to eighteen months, with another eighteen months as an 'improver' in an ordinary factory, and then, if competent, admittance to the trade as a fully-trained worker) provided that (*a*) the trade unions agreed to co-operate, (*b*) it would not cost too much. But as no one knew what attitude the trade unions would take and the scheme undoubtedly would be costly, the committee made no proposals.

Since the Disabled Persons (Employment) Act, 1944, was put on the statute books, bringing with it a highly-developed organization in the Ministry of Labour, a compulsory 3 per cent quota on the larger employers, and a register of disabled persons, the full difficulties of finding suitable jobs for the disabled have been laid bare. But at least a disabled person has had the benefit of a nation-wide system of resettlement behind him. During the heyday of the Compensation Acts he was virtually alone. For, though some employers' organizations were concerned with rehabilitation, the system as it developed through the insurance companies and the mutual aid associations, ignored it.

The weaknesses of workers' compensation were manifest, and complaints grew in volume, if not in range, as the years passed. Proposals to remedy the objections were made from the very beginning, particularly by the trade unions. In some cases they were minor ones and were implemented, e.g. the inclusion of occupational diseases, of family allowances, the reduction of the waiting period; in others the proposals, being more fundamental, such as the introduction of a state-run scheme, were shelved. What was not put forward with any conviction by either side, was any suggestion of abandoning workmen's compensation altogether as a separate scheme, though at the time of the 1939–40 Royal Commission on Workmen's Compensation, some organizations, like the Shipping Federation, wanted to unify the system with the main scheme of health insurance, and to have flat rates of benefit paid whether the illness was due to sickness or industrial injury.

REFERENCES

1. *Social Insurance & Allied Services*. op. cit. p. 36. (1942–3 Cmd. 6404, vi.)
2. *Workmen's Compensation*. op. cit. p. 53. (1920 Cmd. 816, xxvi.)
3. A. Wilson & H. Levy. op. cit. Vol. I. Cap. VII.
4. *Workmen's Compensation*. op. cit. p. 61. (1920 Cmd. 816, xxvi.)
5. D. Potter & D. H. Stansfield, *National Insurance* (*Industrial Injuries*). (Butterworth, 1950.) p. 7.
6. *Workmen's Compensation*. op. cit. p. 56. (1920 Cmd. 816, xxvi.)
7. *Social Insurance & Allied Services*. op. cit. pp. 37–8. (1942–3 Cmd. 6404, vi.)
8. Potter & Stansfield. op. cit. p. 8.
9. A. F. Young, 'Malingering'. *Social Services Quarterly,* Autumn, 1961.
10. *Workmen's Compensation*. op. cit. p. 13. (1920 Cmd. 816, xxvi.)
11. *Social Insurance & Allied Services*. op. cit. p. 279. (1942–3 Cmd. 6404, vi.)
12. Potter & Stansfield. op. cit. p. 7.
13. *Social Insurance & Allied Services*. op. cit. p. 38. (1942–3 Cmd. 6404, vi.)

6

PROPOSALS TO CHANGE THE SYSTEM

A CLOSE examination of the many suggestions that were made during a half century of experience reveals one, and only one, proposal that would radically have altered the system, and that was the demand for some form of state control. During the debate on the 1897 Bill the dangers of leaving the onus on the individual employer were realized, and the suggestion was made that a trade insurance fund should be established to which employers would be obliged to contribute, but this was rejected. When the Farrer Committee met in 1907 to consider whether the General Post Office should provide facilities for insurance under the Workmen's Compensation Acts, the trade unions, who gave evidence, would have welcomed a system of state insurance, but their recommendations were ignored when the report came to be written. At the end of World War I the famous Holman Gregory Committee was appointed with the specific duty of inquiring into the voluntary system of private enterprise compensation, whether it should continue with or without compulsory insurance, whether a state system should replace it, or whether some state control should be superimposed on the existing system. The trade unions came out clearly in favour of a state system on the grounds that the profits then going into the pockets of the insurance companies should be available to the workers. The employers, on the other hand, were unanimously against it because they thought it would be more expensive to them, even though the evidence proved that for every £100 contributed by them to the insurance companies, only £51 went back to the workers in compensation. The committee decided against a state scheme mainly because the existing system was popular with the employers, who preferred private enterprise to state management. Moreover, the employers had declared that any state system would be rigid and slow, and would quickly become inefficient and expensive through lack of competition, an argument that moved the committee. Further, they thought it undesirable for the state to be a party to disputes with workers in circumstances which so frequently led to litigation, and anyway the trade unions were strongly opposed to a scheme that involved workers in contributions to a state fund. This meant that any state scheme would have had to be financed directly out of the taxes, or be paid for by the employers. As the former proposal was unlikely to receive parliamentary support in the climate of the period, this left the onus on the employers. And as they were opposed to it, the committee felt obliged to accept their view. Professor Levy and Sir A. Wilson blamed the committee for the attitude they took, as they felt too much weight had been given to the opinion of the insurance companies and the employers, and not enough to the trade unions and the workers who time and again showed how unfairly the scheme worked. In view of the trade union opposition to any worker-contribution, it is difficult to see what proposal the Holman Gregory Committee could have suggested that would have had any hope of a successful outcome. In the event they advocated state intervention to the extent that all employers should be obliged to insure against the risks of workers' injuries, and that insurance companies should have to work a system in which at least 70 per cent of employers' premiums were paid in compensation to the workers. Compulsory insurance was never implemented (except for mines) and the 70 per cent was achieved for a time by voluntary agreement.

One other proposal the Holman Gregory Committee made was that a Home Office commissioner should be appointed to supervise the operation and application of the Compensation Acts. His powers would have included the supervision of the relevant departments in the insurance companies, the mutual associations, and the self-insurers. He would have appointed medical referees and regulated their duties, scheduled new industrial diseases, and performed several other functions concerning the Acts. Had such an official been appointed, and a department in the Home Office been established, there might have been a much closer supervision of the working of the scheme than proved to be the case in the inter-war years; and the manifold objections to its working might not have reached the proportions they did. However, none of these proposals was implemented.

Professor Levy was himself a strong advocate of state control as a means of more efficient working. He did not agree with the trade unions that the costs of private insurance were inflated by profits, which if abolished would be available for bigger compensation. The high costs of commission and management were the factors which deprived the workmen of larger benefits; and it was to promote savings on these that Levy urged a change in administration. Nor was he in favour of a highly centralized scheme under a single state institution. Instead he advocated a decentralized system of state administration, in which the existing industrial (mutual associations) or social (friendly societies) organizations would be fully utilized – as in the co-operative associations in Germany (Berufsgenossenschaften).

The trade unions continued implacable, both in their denunciation of the way the scheme worked, and in their opposition to a new scheme to which the workers would contribute. They wanted to keep the scheme separate from other social security services, and they preferred the compensation to be related to earnings but, according to Beveridge, they were determined that the employers should pay for it. The employers in their turn said (through the British Employers' Confederation) that if they were to pay all, then the administration must remain in their hands.

Beveridge Proposals

When Beveridge took over from the Royal Commission the sole responsibility for reporting on workmen's compensation, he was also required to consider the other forms of social insurance that had been built up since 1911. His task, therefore, was less circumscribed than his predecessors', and he was able to see the accident scheme against the backcloth of the social insurances in general. Each had been developed piece-meal, with the result that an inconvenient and, in many ways, unjust hotch-potch had resulted. Beveridge conceived it his duty to weave the existing schemes together to make a viable whole, and especially to fill the main gaps in the schemes, and so to modify the principles that a new pattern, more in line with the trend of thought of the second half of the twentieth century, could be developed. He declared that his scheme was not a revolution, but simply a modification of existing schemes. Yet his primary postulates of a national health service and family allowances, both financed out of state funds (though the insurance fund was to make annual payments to the national health service), and his proposals for a national system of social insurance have accomplished such a transformation in the British social services, as to be deemed a 'revolution' by those who have experienced conditions both 'before and after' Beveridge.

It might be thought that anyone so anxious to 'pool risks', to let 'all men stand together', to 'equate benefit with need' as Beveridge was, would have recommended the abolition of a separate scheme for industrial injuries as a first step towards equity. But he did not. Instead, he faced the problem of the separation of risks with all its anomalies of treating equal needs differently, and its administrative and legal difficulties of defining just what injuries were to be treated as 'arising out of and in the course of employment', by using three arguments:[1]

(*a*) Many industries vital to the community were also dangerous. If men were to enter them, and it was essential that they should, they should be assured of special provision if accident or disease overtook them. Further, the claim to compensation ought to be on the basis of past earning, and not on a subsistence minimum as he was to propose for other social security benefits. The argument of special provision, Beveridge considered, was a very strong one.

(*b*) A man being injured at work meant he was injured 'under orders', which made the situation unlike other accidents and diseases.

(*c*) In equity an employer should not be liable for injury to his work people unless he was blameworthy, in which case an action in common law would take care of him. But to make him legally liable for almost every work-accident was wrong. On the other hand, the only way to rectify the employer's position and yet to provide benefit for an employee if an accident or industrial disease overtook him, whether the employee were negligent or not, was to provide a new scheme.

To Beveridge these three arguments were conclusive, and justified his consideration that the retention of a special scheme served a social purpose in providing a guarantee that those who put themselves in danger for the general good of the community, and accepted the danger of injury 'under orders', would receive special recognition and recompense. They were enough for the government too. For when the White Paper on Industrial Injuries was published in 1944, the wartime government endorsed this part of his scheme.

Whether posterity will be disposed to take the same view is hard to say. For on examining the Beveridge arguments, his first point is seen to contain three aspects: (*a*) that dangerous industries required special provision; (*b*) that justice and humanity demanded a guarantee of higher than subsistence rates of benefit to workers injured in dangerous work, and (*c*) that dangerous trades should offer the extra incentive of a specialized scheme of injury pay to obtain labour. Thus the central theme was the danger of certain industries, and the fact that men put themselves at risk in an uncommon way by working in them. Part I of this study has illustrated the truth of the assertion that some industries have been more hazardous than others, and it may well be that part of the ordinary expenses of such industries should be devoted to generous payments to workers who have braved the dangers and been caught by them. It might also be argued that the courage and fortitude of such men should be recognized every week in their wage packets. But that this would be a justification for a generalized work-accident scheme is difficult to grasp. The difficulty becomes more profound when the hazards of everyday life are considered. In Britain injury and death outside the factory and mine have been many times more numerous than within; and the dividing line between the man hurt on his way to work, and the one injured within the factory gates has, at times, been so thin as to be almost imperceptible. In 1906, when workmen's compensation was extended from certain dangerous industries to all industries, the situation was very different, since there were no alternative benefits, but as national insurance against the inevitable risks of life has been extended, the position has become increasingly anomalous and hard to justify.

Beveridge's second argument was one he did not himself wish to emphasize, though many have been moved by it and would claim that because a person succumbed to a danger in which he had been placed by 'order' of authority, he was in a special category, and ought to have special recompense. Against this others would argue that it is unreal to differentiate between that part of life spent 'under orders', and the part not so spent. In a sense, human beings in a highly developed society like Britain could be said to be 'under orders' the whole time, since it would surely be the duty of each one to keep as fit as possible, both for his own sake, and for the good of all. An illness or an injury, whenever or however contracted, would reduce his productive capacity, throw him on the resources of the community and consequently injure the common good. The 'under orders' argument has, moreover, other facets. For the essence of the accident situation, made up as it has been of a complex of dangers not excluding ignorance, carelessness and negligence by all parties, has been too heterogeneous to reduce to the simple formula of 'under orders'. Further, the presence of a special scheme of compensation would appear to have had little influence on those giving the orders, to develop safety devices; nor on those receiving them, to exercise care.

On balance, the implications to be drawn from Beveridge's own arguments are far from favourable to his conclusions and, if the progress of the scheme were to rest on them alone, it is hard to understand how it has continued. But there is a reason, and a very powerful one, why there has been no move to abandon it – and that is the strength of tradition. Workmen's compensation has been part of most workers' armoury as long as they can remember. It has offered a better rate of benefit than sickness insurance, and so long as there is a chance to obtain this higher rate, even if for selected cases only, so long will the scheme be supported. It is in truth a protest against the general principle of fixing national insurance benefit at or below the level of subsistence. Thus the most telling argument is political, and few have wanted to become involved. So when in 1963 the Labour Party presented its new plan for social insurances, it refrained even from discussing the case, and contented itself with the tacit assumption that differential benefits should persist. If and when the political climate changes, the way may open for a more rational arrangement.

Meanwhile a substitute for the ill-favoured workmen's compensation scheme had to be found, and to this Beveridge bent his energies. His first task was to examine the proposals of the disbanded Royal Commission which, with one important exception, he found acceptable. For they had suggested that there should be a pooling of the cost of the scheme, along with the maintenance of as much industrial self-government through the mutual indemnity associations as possible. Secondly, they wanted a special levy on hazardous industries and thirdly, they thought that beneficiaries under the scheme should not be treated differently from others who suffered interruption of earnings (on account of sickness, unemployment) until thirteen weeks had passed.

With the second and third of these proposals Beveridge concurred. He wanted the special levy because of the need to encourage employers in industries of high risk to take special care. He was aware that the case that seemed plausible in 1897 for making each employer bear his own risks broke down in modern conditions, where the whole range of employment was covered, including non-profit-making employment like the domestic and public services, and where the philosophy of the times had changed to one of mutual inter-dependence, with the consequent need to 'stand together'. On the other hand, he said,[2] 'though a high risk of accidents is inevitable in mining, shipping and some other industries, it does not follow that all accidents are inevitable . . .' 'the number and severity of accidents can be diminished or increased by the greater or less care on the part of those who manage industry'. So he favoured a combination of pooling the responsibility with a special charge on certain scheduled industries of high risk. This levy would be based on the amount by which the average cost of compensation in each of the scheduled industries exceeded the average cost of compensation as a whole, and each industry would be expected to pay only two-thirds of the excess, the rest being met out of the fund. Which industries should be the scheduled ones was to Beveridge a matter for negotiation, but he thought mines, quarries, docks, shipping, constructional works and railways were six that would be chosen on the basis of their past record. He thought certain forms of factory work might also be scheduled, like woodwork, metal extraction, ship-building and perhaps parts of the building industry and agriculture.

To give point to the scheme, and to marry financial incentive with accident-free merit, he proposed the establishment of statutory associations in each of the scheduled hazardous industries. These associations would be representative of employers and employees and would, among other things, allocate the extra levy among the individual firms by means of a quota, which would vary according to the accident merit of each firm. Each association would also promote safety and health as well as education and rehabilitation.

On the face of it the special levy linked with the statutory association had some attractive features. It might have ended the British separation between accident prevention and the employers' financial responsibility for accident compensation. On the other hand, the amount of negotiation required by such a scheme, and the opportunities for dispute and litigation inherent in its administration, might have exposed it to some of the same criticisms that were to be the downfall of the old Workmen's Compensation Acts.

With the Royal Commission's proposal to separate the first three months of incapacity from the rest, Beveridge also agreed. He was not prepared to say that payment should be the same as for unemployment or sickness, but he did think it should be at a flat rate, and in no way dependent on past earnings. In this way, 90 per cent of the cases would be dealt with, leaving a bare 10 per cent for the more difficult assessment of medical and financial factors. For this 10 per cent of the cases he was prepared to accept the old method of compensation on the basis of earnings lost. But he insisted that the proportion should be two-thirds of a man's average earnings, with a ceiling as in the old scheme. He was also prepared to accept the lump sum in certain selected cases. As for partial disablement, and benefit for dependents in fatal accidents, they should be linked to a man's previous earnings.

Where he departed fundamentally from the Commission's proposals, as well as from all previous proposals, particularly those of the trade unions, was in his methods of financing the scheme. For he advocated a tri-partite system of insurance, to which not only the employer contributed, but the worker and the state as well. He had already accepted this principle as one that had been tried and proved workable in unemployment and sickness, and he now suggested that industrial injury compensation should be grafted on to his proposed national scheme of social insurance, an institution, he said, implying both compulsion and that men should 'stand together with their fellows'. Thus the principle of selective coverage of personnel, established under the first Workmen's Compensation Act, was to be replaced by the principle of compulsory inclusive contribution by all employed persons, whether white-collared or manual, with no upper income limit.

Though his source of finance was to be so different from that proposed by the Commission, he was not averse to their suggestion of using the insurance offices, the mutual indemnity associations and the friendly societies as means of administering the scheme. He was equally favourable to the alternative idea, that the new government body he had suggested to administer the rest of his social insurance proposals should be used for this purpose too. What he was anxious to avoid was the perpetuation of the court system as the regular means of settling disputes. Instead, he advocated the administrative tribunal, and the appointment of special officers to deal with claims.

Government proposals[3]

When the wartime government came to look at the Beveridge proposals their general reaction was to reject those he had borrowed from the Royal Commission, and accept those that were his own. Their view of the special levy on the employers in hazardous industries was that it was contrary to the principle of 'all standing-in', which Beveridge had made such a prominent feature of his general scheme, and which they accepted. It would, moreover, be an unjust tax on certain industries, which were hazardous by their very nature and not because less care or money had been expended on them. Experiences had shown that the workers' compensation scheme, which in effect was a tax on employment with rebates in the form of a no-claims bonus, had not led to greater care by employers, and consequently Beveridge's argument, that such a levy served a social purpose, fell to the ground. Moreover 'hazardous industries' would be so difficult to define, and so subject to change, that disputes and injustice would be inevitable. Further, to confine these extra payments to employers alone was to ignore the part played by the worker in accident prevention. Thus, while the government wanted to encourage the establishment of joint safety committees wherever they were feasible, and advocated the development of safety schemes under the Factories and Mines Acts, they were not convinced that a special levy would give rise to anything but injustice.

The principle of separate treatment for short – (under 13 weeks) and long-term injury did not appeal to them either. For if a man were paid a flat rate of sickness benefit at the beginning, the whole question of whether he would qualify later for special treatment, because his illness 'arose out of and in the course of his employment', would have to be investigated in the early period. And this would give rise to all the old complaints about anxiety preventing recovery, and the danger of malingering, that had marred the old scheme. Nor did they approve of a system as inflexible as this. Human injury and human recovery were not measured by exact periods of time, but by the nature of the illness and the recuperative qualities of the human being. In consequence, the government White Paper argued, if there was to be a disability pension based on need and higher than ordinary sickness benefit for the long-term case, there should be a similar one in the short term. Thus no one would be encouraged to prolong an illness in the hope of gaining a higher benefit.

By the same token, they eschewed the principle of paying benefit in proportion to earnings. This they did because it was contrary to the declared principles of social insurance, which wanted to relate benefit to need. Further, experience had shown how difficult it was to assess a man's earnings before his accident. And situations could give rise to the anomaly of men, with similar status and employment, and having had similar accidents, receiving dissimilar benefit. The suggestion that a 'notional' earnings figure might be applied was not accepted because it would be fraught with dispute. Nor was the idea of a 'standard rate' for different types of employment any more practicable. The only way out of the impasse, in the government's view, was to concentrate on two features: need, and the degree of disability. Need would be related to the cost of living and the size of a man's family. Disability might be total or partial.

Where the government agreed whole-heartedly with Beveridge was in his general proposal concerning the source of finance and, *ipso facto*, the potential beneficiaries and the method of settling claims. Where he had been uncertain they were clear. No longer should insurance companies and the other private agencies run the scheme. Instead, the government itself would be responsible.

REFERENCES

1. *Social Insurance & Allied Services*. op. cit. pp. 38–9. (1942–3 Cmd. 6404, vi.)
2. Ibid. p. 42.
3. *Social Insurance. Part II. Workmen's Compensation*. (1943–4 Cmd. 6551, viii.)

7

THE NATIONAL INSURANCE (INDUSTRIAL INJURIES) ACT, 1946

THE Bill was introduced in August 1945 and the chief recommendations of the White Paper were enacted the following year.[1] With a few exceptions, persons under contract of service were compulsorily insured against industrial injury. Such exemptions as were made were to be decided by the Minister, subject to appeal at the High Court in certain cases (e.g. matters of law). As the weekly contribution was relatively small, few needed to seek exemption, and most paid willingly, knowing the benefits to be high in proportion to the contribution. There was no longer any limitation on income, type of work or age. If a person was in normal employment, as an employee, he was required to pay, even if she were a married woman opting out of the general scheme of national insurance, or an old age pensioner. Employers contributed in respect of their workpeople, and the state subsidised the scheme. The contributory income in the period after the Act was, on the average, approximately £40,000,000 per year, of which the state contributed about one-fifth (£8,000,000), the rest being divided between the employers' and the employees' contributions.* In a few cases, self-employed persons were included, so that the definition of personnel covered was interpreted fairly widely. A separate industrial injuries fund was to be

* This had risen to over £65,000,000 by 1961, and the Exchequer contribution was £13,000,000.

kept by the Minister of Pensions and National Insurance (as he became in 1953) and the administration was to be undertaken by the normal staff and offices of the Ministry.

The benefits themselves were to be available to insured persons who had incurred injury caused by accident arising out of and in the course of their employment, or had developed a 'prescribed disease', or had suffered a 'prescribed personal injury not caused by accident, but arising out of and in the course of employment provided the disease or injury developed after the appointed day' (5 July, 1948). The formula 'arising out of and in the course of employment' was borrowed from the Workmen's Compensation Acts, not because it was a popular one, but because no better formula presented itself and because, over the fifty years the Acts operated, it was so often interpreted by the courts, that its meaning became reasonably clear and certain. As one compensating officer remarked, [2]'I am convinced that it is better to stick to the devil we know than fly to devils we know not of.' However, though the formula was the same, the position changed, and many were to receive benefit under the new Act, who would not have done so under the workers' compensation scheme. For instance, a claim would often fail under the old scheme because the onus of proof was on the worker to show that an accident not only arose 'in the course of' employment, but also 'out of' it. If there was no evidence either way a claim would often fail, especially in the case of fatalities. But in the new Act, if an accident arose 'in the course of' employment, it was deemed to arise 'out of' it too, unless there was clear evidence to the contrary. Or take the question of travelling accidents, the subject of much dispute under the old scheme. It was laid down (Section 8) that if an accident happened during the employer's time at a place where the worker had a right to be in the course of his employment, then he was entitled to benefit. Thus a messenger boy who had an accident in the street while he was delivering a message for his employer would be covered. If he had one while he was going to work, though it might be in the same street and a similar accident, he would not be covered. If, on the other hand, a worker travelled to or from work on 'special' transport (bus, train, ship) provided by the employer, he would not have been covered under workers' compensation, because there was usually a signed contract not to bring a claim. But the 1946 Act reversed this, and the worker would be covered, even though he could have used other means of transport. So the law was to continue to be uneven in the way it treated travelling accidents, though it was to be more generous than before.

The new Act tackled the problem of a worker's misconduct. The old Acts refused compensation if the accident or injury was due to a worker's own misconduct, unless the injury was very serious, or fatal. This was reversed (Section 8), and an injured person would be covered in the ordinary way, even though he had been disobedient or negligent. This, and certain other matters, were incorporated in the Act itself, leaving a mass of detailed interpretation still to be dealt with by the Commissioners or the Minister, and in some cases by legislation.* The persistence of so many anomalies and complexities gives rise once more to the query as to whether a separate system of benefit is really justified.

Types of Benefit

Although the White Paper disapproved of the Beveridge recommendations regarding short- and long-term incapacity, they were prepared to recommend different types of benefit. So, when the Act came into operation on the appointed day in July 1948, the benefits were:

1. *Injury Benefit*

This was to be paid for a period, not more than twenty-six weeks, during total incapacity following an industrial accident or the onset of an industrial disease. The benefit might be raised by additional allowances for dependents. Though the benefit received by the injured person was to be higher than that of a sick person under the national insurance scheme, that for his dependents was not. There was no question of the injury benefit continuing until the six months had elapsed, if it was clear that a disablement benefit would be more appropriate; and in any case, injury benefit would not be payable to sufferers from the lung diseases of pneumoconiosis or byssinosis, to whom disablement benefit was available from the onset of the disease.

* e.g. In 1961 the Family Allowances and National Insurance Act contained a clause removing anomalies arising out of the 'Common risk' type of injury.

2. *Disablement benefit*

This was to be payable from the end of the injury benefit period, in respect of a loss of physical or mental faculty. This benefit would not be paid on the basis of a person's incapacity to work, and the amount paid would bear no relation to a man's previous earnings. Instead, the example of the Ministry of Pensions in its handling of war victims was used, and a schedule of percentage loss of complete good health was drawn up. Had Professor Levy lived long enough to see this development, he would no doubt have felt some satisfaction that the proposals he put forward with such vigour were accepted. Included in the list was 'disfigurement' which must also have been a source of gratification to those who tried so long to include 'loss of personableness' among the injuries for which compensation was due. If the degree of incapacity were assessed at 20 per cent or more, a weekly pension would be paid. Should a person be regarded as having 100 per cent incapacity, he would receive a pension equal in amount to injury benefit. But, while injury benefit would be paid because a man was unable to work, there was to be no such limitation in the case of disablement benefit. He might thus earn a full-time salary, and receive 100 per cent disablement benefit. The number of such cases was not likely to be large, though the proportion of full-time workers who were to receive disablement benefit at less than 100 per cent has proved to be considerable.

Additional Benefits

Because disablement benefit was concerned with a man's loss of faculty he would receive no allowance for dependents, unless circumstances made it necessary. Also, because there was no connexion between the disability pension and a man's previous earnings, special arrangements have had to be made if he could show that he was obliged to take a smaller income because of his disability. Further, if as a result of his injury he was obliged to employ someone to look after him, or had to go into hospital for a period, other special arrangements were necessary.

These additional benefits were to be very important to the disablement cases. They included *special hardship allowance, unemployability supplement,* and *constant attendance allowance*. Of these by far the most important, numerically, was the special hardship allowance

(Section 14), which sometimes increased the disability pension to 100 per cent, if a man could show his income at work was affected by his injury. The unemployability supplement (Section 13), which could include dependents' benefits, was to be paid if the beneficiary was unable to work because of his loss of faculty, and the condition was likely to be permanent. The constant attendance allowance (Section 15), as its name implies, was paid if a person with 100 per cent disability pension required someone to give him constant attention. Thus a permanently disabled person might receive 100 per cent pension and, in addition, an unemployability supplement, and a constant attendance allowance. If he had to go into hospital while receiving a disablement pension, the pension was to be automatically regarded as 100 per cent, and he would in addition receive dependents' allowances. Thus dependents' benefits were to be available only in respect of the unemployability supplement, or approved hospital treatment if a person were on disability pension.

The Gratuity

If the degree of disablement were assessed at less than 20 per cent, the benefit was to be paid in most cases as a lump sum, varying downwards from a maximum at 19 per cent. The gratuity was the sole remnant of the old workers' compensation lump sum, but, as it was to be paid for minor disabilities, it was regarded as a convenient way of commuting what would have been very small weekly payments. The fact that a gratuity had been paid, however, was no bar to reopening the case should the injured workers' condition deteriorate. In any case, the special hardship allowance might be claimed even by those who had received the gratuity.

It was Beveridge's view that disabled people should not be permanently considered hopeless, and that the national health service, when inaugurated, should be mobilized to maximize a person's health prospects. This view was echoed by the Tomlinson Committee in their report on disablement[3] and has been expressed many times since. Of course, if a man lost his leg, it was a permanent disability. But this did not mean that all the resources of the community should not operate to help him make the most of what was left. Thus there was a tendency, in awarding disability pensions, to make them provisional, in the hope that the physical and mental factors would so improve, that an injured person might regain the maximum capacity that had been left to him. As so many services were by then available (e.g. national health service, Ministry of Labour rehabilitation and resettlement schemes) there was no reason why an injured person's condition should not improve (unless there were positive medical reasons to the contrary), but this did mean that the disablement pension might be reduced if it did. The balance between the incentive to get well, and loss of pay if one did, was therefore still present. But, whereas during the period of the Workmen's Compensation Acts, the possibility of returning to reasonable productivity was often poor, the full employment after World War II offered so much scope to the disabled, that the hope of regaining the status of an employed worker was a mighty incentive for most people.

3. *Death benefit*
This would be payable on the death of an insured person as the result of an industrial accident or prescribed disease. The main beneficiary was the widow who would receive a pension with allowances for children. There were to be benefits for other dependents of the deceased, varying according to the relationship and the extent of the dependence, but strictly limited in number.

Administrative Procedure

Because the old compensation scheme had been so roundly denounced on account of its frequent recourse to litigation, some alternative procedure to deal with difficult claims and disputes was required in the new Act. In consequence a whole section of the Act (Part III) was concerned with the 'determination of questions and claims'. It is not the purpose of this study to describe the Act in detail, but to consider by what principles and methods the new scheme was to be run so that justice would be done to the injured parties, without the abuse of public moneys. It had been Beveridge's recommendation for his whole law of social insurance, that a judicious use of the well-trained civil servant plus a lay advisory committee, helped out by an administrative tribunal, would be sufficient. And as this proposal had been accepted in full by the government, it was a question of what new institutions should be created, and how they should work in industrial injuries cases.

The administration of industrial injuries insurance involved three aspects: legal, financial and medical. The medical side was not normally within the scope of the civil servant, but the other two were. Accordingly, as the new Ministry of National Insurance had been made responsible for administering the scheme, it was necessary to appoint officers at all levels, local, regional and central, trained to assess the legal and financial side of the claims. The Ministry developed 'in-training' schemes to help serving officers to specialize in this work, and issued a mass of memoranda setting out the rules and keeping up to date the decisions on various cases. 'Case law' was thus being developed and made available to those who met the public and made the determinations. Local officers could seek help from regional officers, and decisions were scrutinized, so that there was very little chance of a local officer making a decision that had no precedent, or that had not been approved at a higher level. And as decisions were nationally circulated, the danger of one decision being given at Crewe, and a different one, on the same set of circumstances, at Ipswich, was not very great. Under the old compensation scheme the variety of decisions given by the County Courts (over 400 of them) was a constant source of irritation.

It was also enacted that an industrial injuries' Commissioner and deputies* were to be appointed with legal qualifications (barristers of not less than ten years' standing) to give help where a specially difficult legal point arose. They were to act singly or as a tribunal of three, and might seek the help of expert assessors if necessary (Section 42). In a very limited number of cases the help of the High Court might be sought (Section 37). But it is clear from the Act that courts of law were not to be used save in exceptional circumstances.

Apart from legal interpretations, the actual financial result of an injured person's claim was what would interest him most, and the insurance officers were to be empowered to make the decisions. Should there be disagreement on any point it was open to the claimant, or the officer, to use the local appeal tribunal, a body of three members, composed of a chairman with legal

* One in Edinburgh, one in Cardiff and three in London.

qualifications, one representative of the workers and one other. Medical experts might also sit, either as full members or, more often, as advisers. In practice, the personnel of the industrial injuries tribunal has been the same as for the local appeal tribunal on other national insurance questions, though in theory they were distinct. They were appointed for three years, and could be re-appointed, especially the chairman, though he was required to retire at seventy-two. There was also provision in the Act for certain cases to go to the Commissioner on appeal, otherwise it was the original intention that the decision of the local tribunal should be final.

The medical side of the scheme was relatively simple during the early stages when the injured person was on injury benefit, as the full resources of the national health scheme were at his disposal. From time to time an individual might be asked to present himself for medical examination by the regional medical officers of the Ministry of Health (the Department of Health for Scotland or the Welsh Board of Health) otherwise the matter was left to his own doctor. If, however, the question of a disablement pension should arise, the medical side became crucial and a new structure of local medical boards was inaugurated. The care that was given to planning the boards has been graphically described by Sir Geoffrey King, the first permanent Secretary to the Ministry.[4] At first they thought of letting the Ministry of Pensions do the work, since they had had the experience. Later this idea was abandoned, as there might have been misunderstanding if the civilian scheme were identified too closely with the military. So separate boards were established. And whereas, under the Royal Warrant for War Pensions, the decision was made to rest with the Minister, under the industrial injury scheme it was the other way round, and decisions by the medical boards were to be binding on the Minister, subject to his power, on certain occasions, to refer cases to the medical appeal tribunals.

It was early foreseen that a large number of medical boards would be necessary, and that they would need to be well distributed geographically. Advice on the manning of the boards was sought from the British Medical Association and the Ministry of Pensions, with the result that a large number of local general practitioners were invited to serve. The use of family doctors was thought to have other advantages besides their local availability.

It was anticipated that if a claimant were examined by a local man, he might have greater confidence in the board's decisions, and by spreading the responsibility among a large number of doctors (about 1,700 had been enrolled by 1958), there was more possibility of extending interest and concern about industrial accidents and disease among a wider public. For the same reason, hospitals were asked to provide accommodation on their own premises for the meetings of the medical boards. By 1962, 111 of these boards had been constituted (excluding the eleven special centres for pneumoconiosis cases). As a rule they sat in pairs but, should they disagree, the claimant himself might ask for a third member to be present, when the view of the majority would prevail.

It became the general policy to refrain from reaching a final decision at the first examination, on the grounds that the patient should be given every encouragement to undergo treatment to improve the condition;* thus most first assessments have been provisional.

At this point the question of appeal arises. Not all claimants have an automatic right of appeal. If the assessment was a final one, he might go at once. But were it provisional, he would have to wait approximately two years before going to appeal, unless it seemed obvious to the officers that the case ought to be considered at once.

It was essential that the constitution of the medical appeals tribunals should ensure that they carried conviction both with the claimants and the doctors on the medical boards, whose decisions might be over-ruled. Accordingly, the chairmen were chosen by the Lord Chancellor from barristers of standing and experience, and the two medical members on each tribunal were chosen after consultation with the Presidents of the Royal Colleges in London, and the heads of the University medical schools elsewhere. By 1961, twelve of these tribunals had been established, and though no machinery to co-ordinate their decisions existed, the scheme was thought to work reasonably well. Most of the questions to be decided were medical ones, but if a matter of law arose, such as the interpretation of a regulation, it might go to the Commissioner, who had the power to set aside the findings of the tribunal. Otherwise the decision of the medical appeals tribunal

* Section 25 of the 1946 Act required those on a benefit to take advantage of all available medical facilities. Failure to do so might mean loss of benefit (Section 32).

was final. How they have worked, and in what regard they were held is dealt with in the next chapter which sets out to assess the experience of the first years.

REFERENCES

1. National Insurance (Industrial Injuries) Act, 1946; 9 & 10 Geo. 6. c. 62.
2. D. Potter & D. H. Stansfield, *National Insurance (Industrial Injuries)*. (Butterworth 1950.) p. 19.
3. *Rehabilitation & Resettlement of Disabled Persons*. Cttee. (Tomlinson, Ch.) Report; 1942–3 Cmd. 6415, vi.
4. G. S. King, *Ministry of Pensions and National Insurance*. (Allen & Unwin, 1958.) p. 57.

8

AN ASSESSMENT OF THE 1946 SCHEME'S OPERATION

THE experience of the last fifty years demanded that the new Act should do three things. It should avoid the mistakes of the past; it should provide a viable scheme in which the Beveridge principles of all sharing risks, and all partaking of a certain measure of social security could be maintained; and it should produce a financial position in which the responsibilities of the future would be safeguarded by the rate of contribution, i.e. a funded scheme on the pattern of the commercial insurance of the old workers' compensation type.

To do all this was a leap in the dark. For though some statistics had been gathered, and a certain amount of advice was available from the insurance companies and mutual associations, there was no precise information upon which to work. As the funding of the scheme was a matter of intelligent estimation in the first ten years, so the human problems were a question of guess-work in many instances. As the Annual Report of the Ministry of National Insurance declared in 1952 'the industrial injuries scheme has for the first time provided a means of measuring the severity and extent of the disablement caused by industrial injuries and diseases, and of ascertaining to what extent prolonged disablement continues to affect working capacity. But it will be some years before this measurement can be satisfactorily made, and the relation between physical and mental disability, and industrial capacity established'.

It is known that in the first five years the number of persons insured under the Act, and therefore covered for benefit (since there were no minimum contribution requirements before benefit could be received) was about 20.5 millions, of whom almost exactly one-third were women; and that five years later the number had risen to approximately 21·75 millions, of whom rather more than one-third were women and by 1961 a further 750,000 men and women had been added. This rise of nearly 2,000,000 in eight years was accounted for by increases of nearly 1,000,000 each in the numbers of men and married women. It is also known that claims in respect of rather fewer than 5 per cent of all those at risk were made each year, the number varying from 826,000 in the first year, just over 1,000,000 in 1956, and fluctuating round this figure in the years that followed (998,000 in 1962).[1]

The Benefits

A careful examination of the experience available in each of the benefit groups produced some useful data.

Injury Benefit

It was Beveridge's view that 90 per cent of industrial accidents would be dealt with by this means and, so far, the figures have proved him right. For each year about 800,000 claimants received benefit. The number varied downwards (686,000) in 1957–8, when it was thought the Asian flu epidemic temporarily reduced the number of people at work and therefore at risk, but it has shown a remarkable stability from year to year – a reflection of the obstinate stability of work accident figures. The number of males receiving benefit was about nine times the number of females, which can easily be explained by the fact that men were more likely to be in the dangerous occupations than women. On the other hand the average duration of benefit was higher for women than men, e.g. 31:24 days in 1961. The reason for this disparity, which was echoed in ordinary sickness benefit, might have been partly personal and partly sociological. There is room for further investigation on this question, but it is known that women, in many cases, had domestic responsibilities when they became gainfully employed, and there might be a tendency to continue a period of sick leave until they were well enough to cope with both roles. There were obviously many other reasons, but it would probably be incorrect to deduce that women's accidents were more serious than men's.

Nor was duration of benefit an indication of severity in comparing the different age groups. For the average number of days of benefit rose the older the sufferer was. Between fifteen and nineteen years, the average for boys was about seventeen days, and for girls nineteen days; but in the five years before retirement age the average was thirty-five for men and forty-one for women. Duration of sickness or accident seemed to be as much a matter of personal resilience as actual severity in the injury itself.[2]

On the other hand, comparing industry with industry, there were a few black spots, which showed a high annual loss of time through accidents and disease. Coal mining for men appeared with depressing regularity at the top of the list, and building, transport, engineering and ship-building were good seconds. For women, the industries with the highest loss of time were textiles, and the food, drink and tobacco industries. As we saw in Part I, accidents do not necessarily arise because machines are dangerous, but through the ordinary hazards of falling, or hitting against objects. Yet, the risks of doing this were obviously more serious in certain industries than in others.

Disablement Benefit

Though in numbers the annual recipients of injury benefit constituted the bulk of beneficiaries, the major item of expenditure under the Act was disablement benefit. The average number of new disablement pension awards per year was about 40,000, (29,000 in 1961) compared with 800,000 for injury benefit, but the effect of disablement benefit has been cumulative and therefore expensive and difficult to compute. As we have seen, the award rested on a medical assessment of the degree of disability, and the usual practice has been to make a provisional award for a limited period. Experience has shown that when the case came for reassessment the result might either be (i) the termination of the pension or (ii) its continuation on a provisional basis for a further period when another reassessment would be made, or (iii) its confirmation for life. The cases in the first of these three categories were of three types (*a*) if the disability had disappeared completely the pension was terminated forthwith; (*b*) if it had fallen below the 20 per cent level an appropriate gratuity was substituted for the pension (about three-quarters of the terminations were of this type); or (*c*) if it could be foreseen that the disability would persist for only a short further period the case was disposed of by limiting the currency of the pension to that period – usually from three to six months. Cases in the second category, i.e. in the provisional stage, were not complete until they had either been transferred to category (i) and terminated, or to category (iii) and finalized as pensions.

An analysis of the assessment pattern shows that at first the doctors were reluctant to state finally the degree of disablement that a man's condition represented. Consequently provisional assessments tended to be fairly high. For instance, in 1951, when a sample was taken to see how the scheme was progressing, they found that out of about 86,000 claims (old and new) made during the year, five out of six of the assessments were provisional. This figure should be taken with some reserve, since the number of claims was rising, and certain diseases like pneumoconiosis offered special features which affected the statistical trends. It was rare in this disease for a life assessment to be made until the condition had reached 100 per cent, because prognosis was so difficult. The disease might be stationary for long periods, and suddenly get worse, or it might remain static and the person die of something else. Thus many pensions were stated to be provisional, though in fact they were permanent. As the years have passed, there has been a build-up of life pensions in medical conditions other than pneumoconiosis and, in 1961, when only 29,000 new claims were made, nearly 179,000 disabled persons were receiving pensions. Of these, about half were provisional. From 1952 onwards, though there was an annual rise in the number of pensions paid, the number of provisional assessments remained static (about 70,000). The general pattern of provisional pension seemed to be that the beneficiary recovered completely, or the condition stabilized; deterioration was relatively rare. Of the 47,000 pensions being paid at the beginning of 1951, 30,000 had ceased during the year, and of this number, 2 per cent had died, 25 per cent had no further disablement, and the rest were given gratuities as being under 20 per cent disabled. A further 45,000 new awards (provisional or life) were made during the year.

If a pension survived more than a few months on a provisional basis, it took longer to finalize than had been foreseen. For instance, in 1951 there were still over 8,000 provisional pensions being paid to individuals who had been injured as far back as 1948–9. The uncertainty involved in this state of affairs was liable to have an effect on the disabled man's outlook, and was hardly conducive to peace of mind or stability. On the other hand the average severity of disablement was not abnormally high, being just over 31 per cent (excluding those under 20 per cent). The average for pneumoconiosis sufferers was nearly 40 per cent, and for other prescribed diseases about 41 per cent (T.B. assessments were often 100 per cent, which tended to raise the average here). The majority on pension (about two-thirds) had a 20 to 30 per cent disability, and only very few (about 4 per cent) were so severely afflicted as to receive 100 per cent pension. However, nearly 600 people had been awarded 100 per cent disablement pensions in 1949, and were still receiving them in 1951, a personal tragedy of the greatest magnitude, even though the number represented only 1 in 1,400 of the total number of claims for injury benefit of all types. Further, of every 1,000 pensions being paid in 1951, 346 were due to injuries or disease contracted in 1948, or 1949; and 654 to occurrences in 1950 or 1951. Consequently, though injuries as a whole might not have been serious, many were long-standing. In 1961 half the pensioners (92,700 out of 178,500) had first been awarded a pension between 1948–55. So the effect of long-standing disability was cumulative, and had begun to have a serious impact on the industrial injuries fund.

By no means did all those who made claims for disablement benefit succeed in obtaining them. For in spite of the sifting process, to which a man was subjected immediately after the accident, when he was claiming injury benefit, a number of disablement allowances were refused each year. The main reason for this was the medical decision that no disablement existed. In 1951, for instance, of 86,000 claims submitted (including renewals and new) 8,000 were said not to be disabled at all. But others were refused because it was decided that the accident or disease did not arise out of and in the course of employment.

As the years have gone by, there has been a steady build-up of persons receiving disablement pension, until they far exceeded the number receiving injury benefit at any one time, e.g. in 1961 about 60,000 per week received injury benefit and nearly 180,000 got disablement pensions. Where the pattern in the second and subsequent quinquennia differed materially from the first was in the relative position of the pensions and the gratuities. For, up to 1953, the annual award of pensions rose steadily (38,000 in 1949 to 50,000 in 1953), thereafter the trend was reversed (46,000 in 1954 to 29,000 in 1961). Gratuities, on the other hand, showed a phenomenal rise (22,000 in 1949 to 219,000 in 1961). Whether the annual award of a reducing number of pensions reflected a decline in the severity of disablement, or a toughening in the standards of medical boards, no one knows.

Gratuities

The original intention of these was to separate the minor disabilities (under 20 per cent) from the more serious, and reduce the financial obligation by paying a lump sum. Such a payment would, at first, only be made if the disability was likely to be permanent, and of such a nature as to be more than 5 per cent. Where the scheme differed from the old workmen's compensation 'lump sum' was that it could be examined should a deterioration occur. By 1953 certain important modifications had been made. For one thing, cases with even lower assessments than 5 per cent were included. For another, cases of temporary disability could receive gratuities, making nonsense of the original principle that disability must be permanent. The position became somewhat intricate. A 'permanent' disability was assumed to be one lasting seven years or more, and for this the maximum payment relating to the medical assessment (i.e. from 1 per cent to 19 per cent inclusive) was paid. But, if it was thought a change for the better would occur before the expiration of seven years, the gratuity would be scaled down to one-seventh of the full gratuity for each year covered by the assessment. The net effect has been to increase the number of gratuities awarded to a quite spectacular degree. Gratuities have been given according to a table (e.g. Hancock Committee Report; 1946–7 Cmd. 7076, x), or to the accumulated wisdom of the medical board and, like the pension, were in no way concerned with a man's ability to gain a livelihood. In the light of this, and also in view of the general disapproval accorded to the 'lump sum' in workmen's compensation days, it was all the more significant that the number of gratuities paid each year rose during the period, until by 1961 about 219,000 persons received one, while 179,000 disability pensioners were paid weekly sums. The latter, however, represented the accumulation of thirteen years of the scheme's working.[3]

In the actual numbers of individuals involved, the new legislation made the 'lump sum' far more important than the disability pension. But there has been no outcry. The reason for such a paradox may be twofold. Firstly, there was the right of an individual to have his case reopened if his condition deteriorated, and secondly his right to receive the additional benefits, particularly the 'special hardship' allowance. Neither of these was available to cushion the 'lump sum' under workers' compensation, which might be part of the reason for its unpopularity.

The average gratuity paid did not increase in amount, in spite of the improved scales awarded from time to time. For though the average lump sum in the first quinquennium was about £35 per person, it had fallen to under £30 thereafter, and the total cost of gratuities did not rise, though the total numbers did.

Additional benefits

One of the most novel and important features of the new industrial injuries scheme has been the complex of payments, the 'additional benefits'. It had always been foreseen that, whereas workmen's compensation was founded on loss of earnings, the new scheme, being based on loss of faculty, might mean that a man with a relatively slight injury, and therefore small disablement award, would find himself with a disproportionately severe loss of earnings (e.g. the loss of a finger to a violinist). To offset the inequalities of such a situation, the system of additional benefits was devised. So important had these become, that early in the scheme nearly one-third of the annual expenditure on disablement benefit had gone in this way. In 1951, for instance, of every £100 of disablement expenditure, £40 was spent on pensions, £30 on gratuities, and £30 on supplementary allowances, of which the special hardship one was by far the most important.

Additional benefits were available solely to that minority of occupational accident and disease cases who had been awarded disablement benefit, and were intended to meet extraordinary circumstances arising out of the injury. Against the general risks of life such as unemployment, sickness and old age they did not apply. Should a disabled person have an ordinary illness, or suffer a period of unemployment not connected with his injury, or reach retirement age, he could claim the appropriate benefit under the general national insurance system, while at the same time receiving his disablement pension; and there were arrangements with the National Assistance Board that if he was obliged to seek supplementation, a certain amount of his disability pension would not be taken into account in the 'needs test'.

Special Hardship Allowance

Of them all, this has proved the most popular and the most expensive; and, as it has been directly concerned with loss of earning power, it seems to have given point to the contention of the trade unions before the Beveridge Committee, that any future system of workers' compensation should be based on loss of earnings. The allowance 'can be paid with a disablement pension, or in addition to a gratuity, if the injury or disease makes the claimant permanently* unfit for his regular occupation and incapable of work of an equivalent standard; or if he is continuously unfit for his regular occupation or equivalent work, apart from certain periods (for example an unsuccessful trial return to work) from the time when his injury benefit period ends'.[4] The allowance was calculated on the difference between the standard of remuneration a man would have received in his regular occupation, and the actual wage he was able to earn after the accident. There were limitations, including a ceiling on the allowance itself, as the sum of the disability pension plus the allowance must not exceed the amount a man would have had, had he received the pension at 100 per cent.

It will be seen that special hardship allowances were available to those on gratuity as well as to those on pension. At first it was thought that the gratuity class of the disabled worker would seldom need the extra allowance, and in the early years of the scheme only about one in four of the allowances was given to them. As time went on, and the 1953 Act extended the range of disablement that could attract a gratuity, many more applied for and received

* We saw earlier how this has been modified since 1953.

the hardship allowance, until by 1961 about a third were being paid to recipients of gratuities (39,000).

With this change in pattern went a rapid rise in the number of hardship awards – from 17,000 in 1949 to 118,000 in 1962. The acceleration was due both to the increasing number of persons requiring disablement benefit, and to the unexpectedly high loss of earning power among those with minor handicaps.

Many of the hardship allowances have proved to be temporary. When he first returned to work a man was often not able to reach his former earnings, but rehabilitation and experience of his own disability would frequently correct this, and he would return eventually to his previous earning power. It was noticed that age was a factor, and that the younger workers were more likely to claim the allowances than the older ones. In pneumoconiosis cases, on the other hand, it was seldom that a hardship allowance had to be paid in the early stages of the disease, though a disability pension would be awarded. But the danger increased later and the application for a hardship allowance was almost inevitable. On the whole, there was a fairly rapid turnover of hardship allowance cases, and the Government Actuary has calculated that, of the awards in any one year, only about one-fifth remained payable four years later.[5] Moreover, because hardship allowances were more likely to be needed immediately after return to work, they tended to be associated with provisional pensions more than with life ones.

One other indication of the growing importance of the special hardship allowance was the average rate of the award. Seven-eighths of the allowances were paid at the maximum rate, and this applied to accidents and diseases (including pneumoconiosis) alike, the average amount for all cases being about 95 per cent of the maximum rate. Having regard to the legal limitations on the allowance, the best explanation of the change would appear to lie in the large number of injured who were awarded a low disablement percentage, but who nevertheless were severely handicapped in earning power. Thus the possible injustice inherent in the principle of disablement awards seemed to be counterbalanced by the allowance. That it was not the complete answer was shown by the attitude of the T.U.C. which repeatedly petitioned the Minister for a review of the anomalies, for instance, the loss of promotion prospects because of the accident, and the low rate of the legal maximum. At first, the Minister rejected these requests, partly because he thought it too early to institute a satisfactory review, and partly because he would not wish to tamper with the main principle of disablement award (loss of faculty) by enlarging the scope of the special hardship allowance (loss of earnings), but later he modified his attitude, as in 1961, for instance, when loss of promotion prospects became a ground for granting the allowance.

Other Supplementary Allowances

The number of disablement pensioners benefiting from these has been so small, that successive government reports have made no comment on their application. To the recipients they must have made a substantial difference in the household income. They were paid only in respect of injured persons whose loss of faculty amounted to 100 per cent, and they could be claimed by similar persons who had been awarded workmen's compensation prior to 1948. As the maximum available under these allowances might increase the full disablement pension by over 150 per cent they were an important item. The sum of the pension and allowances might well provide a severely injured man and his wife with as much as the average current earnings.*

(*a*) *Constant Attendance Allowance* was paid where a worker was so incapacitated as to need it. If the workers' wife could act in this capacity the allowance could be paid in respect of her. At the beginning of the scheme about 500 received it, as well as another 500 who were on workers' compensation. The number rose gradually until by 1962 2,360 pensioners were receiving it, including 400 workmen's compensation cases, and 160 sufferers from pneumoconiosis or byssinosis, a number representing little more than one per cent of all the pensioners under the industrial injuries scheme (179,000).

(*b*) *Unemployability Supplement* was available where the injured worker was not qualified (by contributions) to receive sickness or retirement pension, but where, due to industrial causes, he was

* In 1963 the average weekly earnings for a male manual worker were £15 17*s*. 3*d* (October 1962 inquiry) but maximum disablement pension was £5 15*s*., maximum constant attendance allowance was £5, unemployability supplement £3 7*s*. 6*d*., and dependent's benefit £2 1*s*. 6*d*., making a total of £16 4*s*. per week to the severely disabled man and his wife.

unable to work or where earnings did not exceed a very small sum per week. Only very few were in the category; at the beginning about 300 qualified, and by 1962 about 900 were included (200 being workmen's compensation cases). Thus it was of minor importance financially and statistically, but to the unfortunate who came within the category, or who lay just outside it, it was of prime importance. The T.U.C. have drawn attention to the anomaly, that though there has been a doubling of the 'maximum earnings' disregarded in the case of war pensioners undergoing a 'needs test', a similar modification for industrial injuries' sufferers was not available. Thus unemployability was defined at a very low point (raised to £2 per week in 1961), and anyone earning more would tend to make himself ineligible for the full award. Dependents' benefit was also available under this scheme.

(*c*) *Hospital Treatment Allowance* was paid to disablement pensioners during treatment in hospital. At such times the pension was brought up to 100 per cent by means of the allowance and might be supplemented by a dependent's benefit. In 1951 about 400, or one in 200 pensioners, got it for an average of five weeks each, and at an average extra benefit of £7 per person. The number involved seems to have remained constant thereafter.

Thus, of the many allowances available to those on disability benefit, none was of numerical importance except the 'special hardship' one. The fact that so few received the other allowances might have been a reason for congratulation to our health service, in so quickly and effectively returning a worker to a job. Or it might be a cause of concern lest some in need were not aware of their rights.*

Before leaving the area of disablement benefit there remain two categories of sufferers to consider:

(i) The old *workers' compensation* cases. When the industrial injuries scheme was introduced in 1948, it was decided to leave those already on compensation where they were. Accordingly, insurance companies set aside the necessary funds to provide such claimants with a guaranteed weekly sum so long as they were eligible. It is hard to discover the exact number in this position

* The danger of this was reduced by the fact that the allowances were clearly set out on the claim forms. Ministry officials did not hesitate to acquaint a pensioner of his rights if they thought he came within the meaning of the regulations. But as much of their information was, of necessity, available from a man's dossier, it was not known how many slipped through their scrutiny.

in 1948, but ten years later the Ministry[6] gave a rough estimate of 30,000 still receiving compensation, of whom one-quarter were totally incapacitated, and another quarter partially so, but receiving maximum compensation. Besides these, a further 50,000–75,000 were 'latents', and might be expected to claim compensation at any time (if the injury or disease occurred earlier than 1948 this would be their remedy). Of those on compensation nearly one-third who received payment in 1958 had been 'latents' in 1948. Compensation cases do not last for ever, but by 1958 they had become a sizeable body of sufferers, in number equal to nearly one-fifth of those on disability benefit. Yet the basis of their compensation was fixed by the earnings rule, and by the rate of compensation payable in 1948. This situation was so palpably unfair that, in spite of the Ministry's refusal to saddle the industrial injuries' fund with them, some relief of their situation was inevitable. Accordingly, during the period under review several relaxations have had to be made. In 1951, those injured before 1924, and who were still on compensation, were given supplementation from the industrial injuries fund; in 1953, if the unemployability supplement were claimed, dependents' benefit was also available; and in 1956 all compensation cases who were totally disabled and likely to remain so for at least thirteen weeks, irrespective of the date of the injury, were given a weekly supplement out of the fund. In 1962 the position of those injured after 1923 was reviewed, and those partially incapacitated but entitled to pensions at the maximum rate were given an additional allowance. Even so, compensation cases did not participate automatically in any increased benefit rates available to those whose disablement occurred after 1948, nor did they have the right to transfer to benefit under the new Act. The White Paper on industrial injuries had declared that such a transfer, involving a complete reassessment of the claim (on a medical and not an earnings basis), would be difficult, and might lead to more injustice than leaving those injured prior to 1948 to the responsibility of the employer. When the T.U.C. approached the Ministry on the matter in 1958, they were told that the principle of the White Paper continued, and that any relaxation was on grounds of hardship, and was not to be regarded as anything but a charitable act.

(ii) *Pneumoconiosis.* Pneumoconiosis and byssinosis, both being industrial diseases, were covered by special regulations. Persons eligible for benefit must have worked for a prolonged period in industries subject to this risk (e.g. coal mining in the cases of pneumoconiosis and cotton in the case of byssinosis), and when it was proved that the disease was present, a disablement pension was granted. There was no period of injury benefit, and no gratuities were paid. At first, sufferers from byssinosis had to show twenty years' employment in the relevant processes, and were ineligible for benefit until 100 per cent incapacitated, but by 1956 the time of employment was reduced to ten years (as it was for other scheduled diseases), and there was no limitation on the degree of incapacity. As for pneumoconiosis, disablement pension was paid on any condition at or above 5 per cent incapacity until 1954, when the lower limit was abolished, and all sufferers at whatever stage were granted pensions. The number of awards was just over 7,000 in 1949, and rose steadily each year to 48,700 in 1961.

It was difficult to compare the incidence of the disease with earlier experience (in spite of figures published by the Ministry of Fuel and Power since 1943) since so many factors had changed. For instance, diagnosis had greatly improved. The automatic suspension from the job was abolished and many sufferers, who had tried to hide the onset of the disease, came forward to be examined when they knew they would not be obliged to give up their posts. Statistically the effect was dramatic; but it would be improper to conclude that a serious deterioration in the position had taken place. The Government Actuary foresaw an even larger increase in notifications in the 1960's, when the full results of the mass radiography programme for miners, initiated by the National Coal Board, became known. The National Union of Mine workers[7] was naturally concerned about its members, and from time to time expressed dissatisfaction to the government about the working of the pneumoconiosis medical panels, and other aspects of the scheme. Certain amendments were made; for instance, as from August 1958 the officers of the Ministry of Pensions and National Insurance had the responsibility of deciding whether death was due to pneumoconiosis or byssinosis. The advantage of this over the earlier method of leaving the decision to the medical panel, was that there was now a right of appeal to the local tribunal, and to the Commissioners as in other industrial injuries.

Special hardship awards for pneumoconiosis patients have tended to be delayed, as the disease is slow to develop. Only later would a man find himself unable to earn what he did at the onset, and be obliged to seek supplementation. This also was reflected in the figures. For by 1958, it was found that two out of three of those awarded pensions before 1954 were receiving hardship allowances, while fewer than one in four of those diagnosed in 1954, or later, received supplementation. It has been estimated that, after five years of the disease, about one in two of the sufferers was eligible for a hardship allowance.

Death

Though the number of accidents remained obstinately high, and the number of deaths through industrial causes seemed to keep to a fairly constant figure, the absolute number of deaths compared with the loss and suffering of injured and diseased workers did not appear so serious. For instance, comparing three-quarters of a million annual awards of injury benefit since the scheme started, with just over 2,000 death awards seemed to make the latter relatively trivial. To view it thus would be a great mistake, since death is irretrievable, and affects the lives and the hopes of the family, as well as the potential productivity of the firm. And when it is known that a proportion of the deaths were unnecessary, the community's loss and the community's responsibility became all the greater.

The arrangements for death benefit under the 1948 scheme were to award a pension to the widow, which she retained permanently unless she remarried, in which case she might receive a gratuity, and to other relatives (e.g. mother of deceased) who could prove financial dependence. In practice few pensions other than to the widow and children were awarded. In 1949, 115 persons other than the widow and children were awarded pensions in respect of the death of a wage-earner, a number which rose to 482 in 1961. As the number, in certain cases, was cumulative, it can be seen that few relatives other than the spouse have been given awards. Whether this was due to their lack of dependence on the dead person, or whether to a stern interpretation of the Act, it is hard to say. There appear to be no publicly recorded instances of relatives protesting against the decision, and one can only assume, for want of evidence to the contrary, that the system worked well.

An average of 300–400 widows remarried each year, with a dowry of around £100 each, and the rest remained on pension, involving an annual increase of more than a thousand. At the beginning of 1949, 851 widows received the weekly pension, rising to over 20,000 by the end of 1961; and the number of dependent children rose from a few hundreds to 14,000. The cost of death benefit for widows and children, being cumulative like the disability pension, also rose from under £160,000 to over £4,000,000 in 1961, or about 5 per cent of the total outgoings of the fund. It is clear that, as the number of deaths through accidents at work was over 2,000 a year,* only about half can have had a dependent spouse or one who remained dependent for life. As far as the fund was concerned, this part was the least expensive item, compared with the seriousness of the accident; but, in the light of the relatively small numbers involved, it would not be difficult to make out a case for increased benefit in this sphere.

General Financial Provisions

In the interests of convenience, the contributor paid for his national insurance and his industrial injuries benefit on one and the same stamp, but the funds themselves have been kept entirely separate. The industrial injuries scheme followed the traditions of its predecessor, workmen's compensation, and arranged for the accumulated expenses of the future to be met by high contributions from the beginning. It was decided to do this, rather than adopt a short-term policy and make a reassessment, say every five years, because, it was claimed, expenses would rise and it would have been so hard to explain why contributions were being changed when benefits were not. Accordingly, the long-term method was used, and the excess of income in the early years was invested to provide a fund that would yield an income large enough to meet the expenditure of the next forty years, when the full charge of the long-term liabilities developed.

Estimating the probable outgoings of a scheme like this was obviously very difficult, since no one knew what the expenses

* This represented the total number, and was more than three times the number reported by the chief factory inspector (see Part I, p. 7) as having been killed.

were likely to be. Income did not offer the same obstacles, as the numbers entering industry were fairly accurately known for fifteen years to come, and could be estimated with reasonable reliability for longer periods. On the inception of the scheme, the number of contributors was around 20,500,000, ten years later it was 21,750,000, and the estimate for the end of the century was a little over 24,000,000.* The income therefore was likely to be stable, unless important changes in contribution rates were made. Weekly payment has been made by all employees under contract of service, and their employers and the Exchequer have supplemented these combined payments by grant-aid equal to one-fifth. In the first full year of the fund (1949–50) the total income (including interest) was £37,000,000 and by 1960–61 was about £90,000,000. However, the important item that concerned the health of the fund was the accumulated surplus, which by 1954 had reached £108,000,000, and by 1962 was £288,000,000.

Outgoings, on the other hand, could not be foreseen with such certainty. No one knew what the disablement scheme and widows' pensions were likely to cost and, since it was an expense that would grow, there was a real danger that there would not be enough in the fund to meet the peak demand when it arrived. Accordingly, in his first quinquennial report, the Government Actuary was pessimistic about the future solvency of the fund, unless outgoings went down, or contributions were raised. By the time the second quinquennial report was available a much brighter picture had emerged. For though the benefit rates had increased by 25 per cent (National Insurance Act, 1957) contribution rates had gone up by 50 per cent, leaving a fairly comfortable balance in favour of the fund. Moreover, the balance of expenditure had altered to the fund's benefit. The disablement benefit, its major item, was showing a change of pattern, as a result of which the ultimate number of disablement pensions in payment in the years ahead would be considerably smaller than was previously estimated. Thus, instead of the fund running into difficulties when the initial years of large surpluses were over, the position at the end of ten years seemed likely to be far more rosy, and the prospect of continuing surpluses seemed assured. In the light of this it was decided in 1961 to lower the contributions

* The forecast of population changes made by the Registrar-General in 1963 would probably alter this estimate.

(but they increased again in 1963 when scales of benefit were improved).

One other financial provision may be alluded to – the Colliery Workers' Supplementary Scheme. The Act (1946) allowed for the registration of schemes of supplementary financial benefits, provided the industrial injuries fund and the Treasury were in no way contributors to them. The only scheme recognized during the period was that of the miners, and though it was not allowed to compete financially with industrial injuries benefits, being only about one-third of the rate, its benefits did rise as the statutory benefit rates themselves increased. While this was the only recognized supplementary scheme, it was not the only one in the field, and many friendly societies as well as private firms provided supplementation of one sort or another to those injured at work. It is not quite clear what the positive benefits of registration can have been; and since the miners were the sole body to take advantage of the provision in the Act (Section 83), the advantages were evidently not apparent to others either.

Appeals

No assessment of the scheme is complete without some reference to consumers' dissatisfaction. This can best be measured by an examination of the nature and quality of the appeal machinery, and the frequency with which it was used. The first distinction to be made is between the medical and the non-medical functions.

Medical

One of the main complaints about the Workers' Compensation Acts had been the operation of the medical boards. It was said that the worker was at a disadvantage when faced with an examination by high-powered medical men appointed by the insurance companies. It was alleged, that these men naturally favoured the side that paid them, and that the benefit of the doubt would be given to the insurance company and not to the injured man. Such allegations cannot possibly be made against the new medical boards and tribunals and, as we have seen, the Ministry made every effort, when constituting the panels, to ensure justice and general acceptability, as well as professional competence. Yet the rate of appeal remained at a steady level and, some might say, a high one. In 1952 for instance, out of nearly 222,000 medical examinations for disablement benefit, there were just over 13,000 appeals (including those brought by the Minister). Crude comparisons of this type would set the rate of appeal at just under 6 per cent. However, as many of the examinations were first ones, resulting normally in a provincial assessment, and as claimants had no right to appeal until their provisional assessment had lasted two years, or they had received a final assessment, the comparison might be misleading. It is difficult to deduce from the published figures what proportion of those examined by the medical boards had the right to appeal. But if it is assumed that all those concerned in first examinations, about half the total, had no right to appeal, then the rate of appeal by those who had rose to around 12 per cent. During the period under review the proportion remained about the same, though the numbers increased (in 1961 there were over 320,000 examinations, and about 20,000 appeals). Thus in spite of growing competence on the part of the boards, and increasing public expenditure on the health services, the proportion of those dissatisfied with the medical findings did not fall.

A breakdown of the total number of appeals indicated that approximately three claimants appealed to every one case brought by the Minister. It was understandable that applicants might sometimes feel dissatisfied at the findings of the medical boards, but that the Ministry should do so too was not so apparent. The position is all the more remarkable considering the numbers involved, e.g. in 1952 the Ministry brought 3,000 cases, and in 1958 the number had risen to nearly 6,000 (it was under 5,000 in 1961). In fact, over the period, there seemed to be a tendency for the ratio of claimant and Ministry appeals to rise slightly in favour of the Ministry. It would be wrong to explain this state of affairs as a persistent attempt by Ministers of the Crown to save public money at the expense of the disabled. On the contrary it was clear from the decisions in the claimants' favour that very many cases must have been brought because the officers of the Ministry thought the medical board ruling was unfair to the men.

This raises the question of the result of the appeals. If, prior to 1948, the dice were loaded against the worker, this can hardly have been the conclusion later. For about 40 per cent of the claimants' appeals were settled in their favour (it was 35 per cent in 1961), and even those brought by the Minister showed an average of 30 per cent in the claimants' favour. Medical diagnosis and prognosis are notoriously difficult matters. And when two doctors are asked to assess the point on the percentage scale at which the disablement should rest, and when this point becomes the basis of payment, it is understandable that many claimants have left the board-room with a growing feeling of dissatisfaction, which led some of them to seek further advice. It can be argued that as nearly 90 per cent decided to accept the findings there was not much wrong with the system. It can also be said that the fact that the machinery of appeal operated, meant that the disgruntled man had a safety-valve. Further, because the appeal tribunal reversed the medical board decision in so many of the cases, justice was seen to be done. This is probably the reasonable way of looking at the matter. Yet when as many as one in nine cases was reconsidered by another team, and when the proportion remained fairly steady over the years and the findings in favour of the claimants were high, there could be no grounds for complacency.

On the other hand, it is pertinent to inquire what safeguards were employed by the state against the individual. During the early part of his illness, a man received injury benefit because he was too ill to work. All the resources of the national health scheme were available, so that he could be made well enough to go back to work. It was no reflection on the family doctors or hospitals involved that the Ministry required a certain number of claimants each year to be examined independently by the regional medical officers of the Ministry of Health. The number so referred increased from about 40,000 to over 120,000 in the period. The results of this check were startling. The proportion incapacitated for work was found to be only about 40 per cent of those examined. Of course it is likely that only those who were suspected of malingering were sent for independent examination, and they represented, in any case, only between 5 and 10 per cent of the total number of claimants (about 800,000 per year). But that more than half the referred claimants were found to have been quite able to work was a serious matter. A closer analysis of what happened has been illuminating. Of every five claimants examined, approximately two were too ill to work, one had already recovered, one was thought to be not incapacitated, though there might be some doubt whether he could go back to his old job, and one did not attend the examination. One can only assume his non-attendance meant he had recovered, since the Ministry offered transport where necessary.

The medical safeguards against the abuse of the system have been reasonably comprehensive and, from the evidence, necessary. So it was not surprising that the number of referrals to the Ministry of Health doctors rose each year.

Non-medical matters

The 'statutory authorities' (the officers, tribunals and Commissioner) had to decide whether a claim could be accepted. In doing so they had to feel their way through a mass of regulations and 'case' decisions. For instance one man, suffering from dupuytren's contracture, worked at a job which involved the hacking of wood with a knife. After several months of this his wrist was practically unusable, and he claimed that his job had made it so. He lost his claim, because it was said that the condition did not arise through an 'accident' or 'incident' at work. It was undoubtedly made worse by the 'process' of his work, but that was another matter. Another man suffered an eye injury, due to his having to unload bricks in a strong wind. The officer, in allowing the claim, had to ask himself whether this man was exposed to a special risk because of his work, or whether it was an Act of God which might have happened to anyone. In the case quoted there did seem a risk in the employment, and so the claim was allowed. But had circumstances been different, the result might well have been the reverse.

In spite of difficulties, such as the above, around 1,000,000 claims were decided one way or the other each year, and claimants could either accept the determinations or appeal against them. If they appealed, the onus was on them to show that the balance of probability was on their side, and some 200 tribunals sat regularly to assess the arguments in the light of the regulations, the most knotty cases being sent to the Commissioner. Compared with the 10,000 to 15,000 (claimant) appellants against the medical findings each year, it might be thought the annual 6,000 cases brought to the local tribunals was very small, and that in consequence there was general satisfaction with the determinations. There is no doubt but that the fairness and competence of the officials were widely recognized, but it would be manifestly untrue to suggest that the mere absence of challenge denoted complete approval. Many felt aggrieved because they knew their physical weaknesses were made worse by being at work, and they thought they ought to have had benefits. But they also knew how complicated were the regulations, and how difficult it would be to prove that their particular case came within the meaning of the Act. The Commissioner, aware of the problem, has published his findings from time to time, so that gradually a body of case law on industrial injuries is being created, though this does not make the position any easier for the ordinary claimant to understand.

The results of the local tribunals' work showed about 40 per cent in favour of the claimants, which was similar to the medical appeals. Of the 600 cases sent annually to the Commissioner, the decisions were slightly less favourable to the claimants, being about one in three.

When the Franks Committee[8] reviewed the various administrative tribunals in 1957, the local tribunals for industrial injuries cases were commended, and were 'generally regarded as having operated smoothly for many years' and in consequence 'no structural changes are called for'. A few minor modifications were suggested, such as the general right to appeal to the Commissioner without the chairman's approval. Otherwise, the normal practices of the industrial injury tribunals, such as public hearings and representations of the claimants by a lawyer (with the chairman's consent), were recommended as suitable for extension to the other tribunals under the National Insurance Acts.

After such high-placed acclaim, it was something of a shock when *The Times*[9] published a series of letters criticizing the working of the tribunals. In these letters Mr. L. J. Sapper, Deputy General Secretary, Post Office Engineering Union, and Miss K. M. Oswald* (herself a member of the Franks Committee) complained about the increasing formality with which the tribunals were being conducted, and the growing complexity of the regulations and case law which had to be unravelled. Both these officers were in a position to know what was going on, and their comments must

* National Secretary of Citizens Advice Bureaux.

therefore be treated with the utmost respect. From their remarks it was clear that, without help, a claimant was unlikely to be able to state his case adequately or to understand the reasons for a decision. For though the trade unions provided a service for their members, large numbers of injured workers, not being trade unionists, had no right to call on the officials for advice. Moreover, the tribunals had sometimes given the impression of conducting a prosecution, in which the claimant was obliged to stand up to cross-questioning, as if he were in the witness box at a trial. No wonder, it was alleged, a man who conducted his own appeal might all too often feel himself alone and unprotected in an inimical atmosphere. The correspondence asked for a return to the 'friendly and informal' approach promised by the government spokesmen when the national insurance legislation came into force in 1948.

The development of the judicial procedure, though unfamiliar to the applicant, may in the long-run have operated in his favour, and in the interests of greater justice. Sir Geoffrey King,[10] reflecting on the high proportion of industrial injuries appeals to the Commissioner compared with the total number of such cases, accounted for it by pointing out the greater legal complexity of the industrial injury scheme compared with national insurance in general. The answer to legal complexity is not to be found in friendliness and informality in themselves, but in the method evolved over centuries of experience by the ordinary courts of law, in the rules of evidence, and the help and advice of the trained legal mind. It is the generous implementation of the Legal Aid and Advice Act, 1949, to cover free aid to those seeking redress in administrative tribunals that is needed, if justice and humanity are to be served in these tribunals.

If the scheme has not operated without the individual being aggrieved, what of the state's complaints against the individual on matters that were non-medical? The Ministry has had at all times the power to prosecute those who failed to pay their contributions or those who, having received benefit, behaved fraudulently. The number of prosecutions for non-contribution was fairly large (about 8,000 a year) but fraud was remarkably infrequent. In the nineteenth century, it was not uncommon for people to inflict wounds on themselves in order to live a life of idleness, finding subsistence by begging from the public. There has been no evidence since 1948 that people have manipulated accidents in order to live at ease on industrial injuries benefit. On the contrary, of the few cases brought to court each year (an average of eighty-five, ninety-five in 1962), the main type of offence was to draw benefit (injury benefit) while going to work, and failing to disclose a change of physical circumstances when on disablement benefit. That there was fraud, not brought to open prosecution, cannot be denied in face of the results of the medical checks on those obtaining injury benefit, but as prosecuting policy has not been unduly altered, the abuses were evidently not serious ones.

Administration

When Beveridge reviewed the workmen's compensation system, one aspect, which he found both puzzling and indefensible, was the cost of administration on the part of the insurance companies. An average cost of 19 per cent of income needed to be pruned, he averred. No analysis of the working of the industrial injuries scheme would therefore be complete without some inquiry into this aspect. In crude figures the annual expenditure on administration increased from just over £2,000,000 to over £6,000,000 a year during the period. This would doubtless be accounted for by the changes in the value of the pound, and would therefore be of little significance. Comparison between the total amount spent on benefits and the cost of administration showed that, in the year 1949–50, about £12,000,000 went in benefit, rising in 1961–62 to nearly £60,000,000. On this basis, expenditure on administration merely kept pace with expenditure on benefits, and averaged about 15 per cent. No comparison can be made with Beveridge's calculation, but having regard to the complexity of the industrial injuries scheme, it cannot be administered 'on the cheap'.

Apart from the cost, another complaint about the administration raised by Beveridge, was the relationship between workmen's compensation and the other social insurance and welfare schemes sponsored by the government. He was impressed by the apparent separation between them; and by the way those in need were shuttled from one office to another in search of relief. He thought there was a case for the insurance and welfare offices being housed in one building in each locality, so that a person on disablement compensation, for example, could sign on at the Labour Exchange, consult the national insurance officers and apply for national assistance without long journeys between each operation.

The idea was seriously considered when the new schemes were started in 1948, but as Sir Geoffrey King[11] related, the project would have involved so extensive a building programme, that it was quite impossible under the post-war stringency. In 1953, however, an experiment was tried where two departments (Ministry of Pensions & National Insurance and Ministry of Labour) happened to share the same building. The staff was made interchangeable, though the two managers were each made responsible for half the staff. It might have effected economies had the work fluctuated in each department, so that the slack in one coincided with the boom in the other. As this was not so, it could not claim even that advantage. On the other hand, it produced difficulties of its own, particularly in management. As Sir Geoffrey remarked 'the range of work in a combined office can be very wide indeed, and may well be too wide for one man to supervise'. So, after a year, the experiment was abandoned.

The administration of each branch of national insurance and family allowances in a limited number of specialized offices was considered, but rejected because, though it would have been administratively convenient, it did not give the public the service they expected, and to equip each local office to deal as far as possible with every kind of national insurance business seemed the best policy. This did not prevent the sharing of offices. For, by 1961, more than half the 827 national insurance offices were shared by the Ministry of Labour, the National Assistance Board or another Ministry, and in several employment exchanges inquiries about national insurance could be made. But, in general, each insurance office was the unit responsible for the full range of industrial and other national social insurance work, the complexities of which may be imagined. As Sir Geoffrey King has recorded, when the appointed day arrived, it meant 'the instruction of a thousand local officers in the intricacies of a subject that had baffled so many learned judges'. The subject was to become no less baffling, and the instruction of new staff no less intricate.

Summary of Accomplishments

The examination of the first few years' working leads one back to the principles on which the scheme was founded. Earlier (p. 108) these were said to be three in number: (1) that the mistakes of the past should be avoided; (2) that the Beveridge principle of 'all in together' should be implemented: (3) and that the scheme should be 'funded'.

Mistakes of the past

(*a*) *Employers' responsibility.* The complaints that employers were not obliged to insure against workmen's compensation, and were not made acutely conscious of their duty in accident prevention by the scheme have only been partly met. To a large extent their responsibility for accidents to their workers was reduced, in the sense that they were no longer wholly liable for compensation. Instead every employee knew that he was covered by contributory insurance which was an obligatory payment for all Class I workers and their employers.

(*b*) *The average wage theory.* The new Act set out to abolish this as a basis of payment for accidents or diseases arising out of employment. On the whole this has been accomplished and new bases of payment have been evolved. Yet it is significant that the 'special hardship allowance', based on wage-loss, grew in importance as each year passed, until more than half the disabled pensioners were receiving one. This experience has shown that no injury compensation scheme could operate without some regard to the level of a man's wages. The real difference lay in the spirit in which it was given. The old idea that a man should be asked to bear half the risk of injury at work was abandoned in favour of a more humane approach. For even though a man might have a minor disability it could result in a major loss of wages, and for this there ought to be, and was, some form of counter-balance.

(*c*) *The lump sum* was for a long time a serious bone of contention. But it was not abolished by the new legislation. Of 1,000,000 claims that were considered each year, more than one in ten resulted in a lump sum (gratuity) being paid. Once again, it was the reason for paying it that made the difference. Under workmen's compensation the lump sum was a way of capitalizing a responsibility, no matter how severe that responsibility was. The gratuity, on the other hand, was never paid if the worker was wholly incapacitated by his injury, but was the compensation for minor disablement alone. Furthermore, proved loss of earnings on account of the injury attracted the additional weekly sums associated with the special hardship allowance, and the gratuity might be reconsidered if the condition deteriorated. Only with these provisos, one suspects, was the lump sum system workable.

(*d*) *Unfairness in medical assessment* was often alleged, and the cause was laid at the door of the employer and the insurance company. The medical boards could not be criticized in this way, yet thousands of claimants appealed each year against the medical assessment for disablement pensions, so discontent could hardly be said to have been abolished.

(*e*) *Litigation* was abused. The original intention of the Workmen's Compensation Acts was to resolve disputes in a 'friendly and informal way', but, in fact, resort to civil procedure was all too common, and fear of litigation became the nightmare of the injured. Disputes under the National Insurance (Industrial Injuries) Act were not to be decided in ordinary courts of law either, but by machinery which might, in the long-run, be less satisfactory than an open court. It is significant that the sponsors of the new scheme in Parliament claimed that difficulties would be ironed out in a 'friendly and informal' way, but within ten years protests were being heard that this was not happening. It is vital to keep a sense of proportion about these protests. There was no evidence that officials at the Ministry, or tribunals, or the Commissioners themselves, were often 'dogmatic in their dealings with an applicant' or that proceedings often 'possess all the formality of the High Court'.[12] It was probably inevitable that formality would increase in any scheme as complex as both these have proved to be.

(*f*) *Malingering* was little heard of, because it was an unacceptable word in the second half of the twentieth century.[13] The antidote for whatever it stands for was built into the scheme through the system of medical checks, and the power of the Ministry to sue suspected persons for fraud. When the employers were personally responsible for compensation, they were on the look-out for any intention to deceive, and spoke and wrote about its prevalence at great length. There was no evidence that 'malingering' had either increased or decreased since the Second World War.

(*g*) *Costs of administration* were still fairly high. Comparisons with those of the private insurance companies would be impossible, since the schemes were so different. But it would be idle to imagine that any compulsory insurance, affecting so many individuals and involving such intricacies of legal and factual interpretation, could be adequately managed without an expensive administration.

2. *The Beveridge principle of 'All in together'*

This has not been so widely applied as in some of the other national insurance schemes. It could be argued that Class III contributors, not gainfully employed, could not logically be insured against accident or disease contracted at work. But why Class II contributors, the employers and self-employed, were omitted (except in certain cases) it would be difficult to say. They were obliged to contribute through taxation and the employers' levy. They were likely to sustain accidents and contract scheduled diseases. There seemed little reason why they should not be included in the compulsory insurance. Otherwise, all employed persons under contract of service have been included, even married women, certain widows and people at work over pensionable age. A few who were not ordinarily included in Class I, such as some sea-going personnel, were covered. In spite of the omissions from the scheme, the fact that well over 20,000,000 were paying their contributions each week indicated that the Beveridge principle of universality had been applied in a way that would have seemed absurd for the workers' compensation scheme.

3. *A 'Funded' Scheme*

The state was under no obligation to build up a fund. It could have made use of current contributions supplemented by taxation to meet the annual outgoings of the scheme. In a sense this method has certain attractions. (*a*) It would have maintained the contributory principle which is acceptable and popular in the twentieth century because it implies the right to benefit and not a charitable dole from the state. (*b*) There would have been no necessity to relate contributions to the requirements of the fund in forty years' time. For though contributions have been low in the first years of the scheme because of its limited coverage, there may come a time when other disablement risks (e.g. through crimes of violence or accidents at home or in the street) are added, making contributions correspondingly large. It is conceivable that the contribution requirements might ultimately be too large for the ordinary man to meet. (*c*) It would not be worried as a 'funded' scheme necessarily is, by the problem of inflation, which involves the difficulty of maintaining appropriate rates of benefit when the value of money changes as rapidly as it has done since the Act was passed. (*d*) In any case, a government pension scheme would be expected to pay benefits commensurate with the standard of living of the period. In an age of expansion this is difficult to achieve without supplementation. (*e*) The Phillips Committee in 1954,[14] facing the problem as it affected old people, expressed some anxiety about the economic effect of the building up of a separate fund by the state to meet the future requirements of the aged, in case the very objects of a modern industrialized state – to promote the growth of productivity – were put in jeopardy. Subsequent arguments* have tended to stress the other view, that the build-up of a large state fund would have a beneficial effect on investment and on the economic progress of the country.

Clearly no private insurance company could expect to stay solvent unless provision were made for future expenditure, and in consequence the workmen's compensation schemes, organized by the insurance companies, were 'funded'. This was not necessarily true of the 'mutual associations' or of the 'self insurance' schemes, which some firms operated. So if the industrial injuries scheme had not been 'funded' it would not have been without precedent. On the other hand, the operation of unemployment insurance in the inter-war period, and of the retirement pension since 1948, have attracted considerable criticism,[15] because the appropriate funds were over-spent, and the element of insurance was thereby reduced and state relief increased. The White Paper on Industrial Injury Insurance in 1944 did not even argue the issue, so self-evident did it seem that the fund should be actuarially viable.

* Especially those of the Labour Party in their plan for a national superannuation scheme in the 'fifties.

In practice then, the contributions have been fixed on a scale that was intended to build a fund large enough to meet the heavy commitments of the future, when outgoings for disablement pensions and allowances will have reached their maxima. Since there was no counterpart in previous legislation, and therefore no firm basis for estimates of expenditure, the Government Actuary in his first quinquennial report described his experience as 'financially, something of an adventure into the unknown'.

There remains one other group of problems to investigate, one that is far-reaching in its repercussions. For every decision the administration has made, every case that is said to come within the meaning of the Act, might lead the injured man to sue for damages, and his employer to the Court charged with a civil offence. The development of 'alternative remedies', the changes that have been wrought in the theory and practice that surround them, and a social assessment of the whole policy of this aspect of civil law become the subject matter of Part III.

REFERENCES

1. National Insurance (Industrial Injuries) Act 1946. Reports by Government Actuary on 1st and 2nd Quinquennial Reviews; 1954–5 (22), vi; 1959–60 (300) xvii.
2. Ibid. Table G.
3. 1962 Ministry of Pensions and N.I. Annual Report. (1962–3 Cmd. 2069.)
4. 1952 Ministry of National Insurance Annual Report. para. 114. (1952–3 Cmd. 8882, xiv.)
5. National Insurance (Industrial Injuries) Act, 1946. First Quinquennial Review, para. 7; 1954–5 (22) vi.
6. Trades Union Congress. Annual Report of General Council 1959. Sect. D.
7. T.U.C. Annual Report 1960.
8. *Administrative Tribunals & Enquiries*. Cttee. (Franks, Ch.) Report, paras. 167–78. (1956–7 Cmnd. 218, viii.)
9. *The Times*, March 6–9, 1962
10. G. S. King, *Ministry of Pensions and National Insurance*. (Allen & Unwin, 1958). p. 89.
11. Ibid. p. 127.
12. *The Times*. Letter by L. J. Sapper, 6. 3. 1962.
13. A. F. Young, 'Malingering'. *Social Services Quarterly*, Autumn 1961.
14. *Economic & Financial Problems of the Provision for Old Age*. Cttee. (Phillips, Ch.) Report, paras. 135–9. (1954–5 Cmd. 9333, vi.)
15. I. Macleod & J. E. Powell, *The Social Services, Needs and Means*. C.P.C. Research Series, 1952.

PART THREE
Alternative Remedies

9

THE COMMON LAW

PROFESSOR LEVY remarked[1] 'the common law in England has always given a measure of protection to workmen against the torts of their employers'. It has not done so without considerable modification, as the social and economic fabric of society has changed and case law itself has built up a situation very different from its earlier appearance. Nor is common law the only ground on which a worker may bring a case against his employer. For, since the first Factory Act in 1802, a body of statutory duties has been enacted, which places upon the owner of premises, and the employer, the obligation to do certain things. Thus, whereas in common law cases it is necessary for the plaintiff (in this case the worker) to prove negligence on the part of the defendant (the owner), in breach of statutory duties there is no such necessity.[2]

The common law of tort in this connexion rests on the doctrine of care.[3] This means that, when two people are so closely and directly related that the activities of one of them may involve an appreciable risk of injury to the other, then a general duty of care rests on the one who pursues the activities. Employer's liability to their workpeople has been found to come within this category, though whether solely within the category of tort has not been specifically decided,[4] since employers and workers are assumed to have entered into a contract with one another, and the law of contract has often been cited in the past to offset the law of tort (e.g. contracting-out clauses in which the worker undertook not to bring an action against the employer in case of injury. This was said to have been a frequent method of avoiding the requirements of the Employers' Liability Act 1880).

The concept of 'care' is clearly a matter of judgment and not of an 'absolute' standard. It implies[5] 'not doing something which a reasonable man, guided by those considerations which ordinarily regulate the conduct of human affairs, would do; or doing something which a prudent and reasonable man would not do'. Such a definition of 'care' bristles with difficulties and has been differently interpreted as changes in the climate of opinion occur. However, even as early as 1856, it was refined into three principles (Alderson B. in *Blyth vs. Birmingham Waterworks Company*):

(*a*) The magnitude of risk. This should mean that the greater the risk, the greater the care.

(*b*) The practical possibilities. Thus a balance has to be drawn between the possible risk involved in an action and the expense, effort and frustration in refraining from such an activity. For instance, it would be palpably unreasonable to shut down a whole factory because of a minor electrical fault in the installation, even though there might be some risk at the seat of the fault.

(*c*) General and approved practice. If certain safety precautions are known and used, it would be regarded as the duty of a careful employer to use them. There are obvious pitfalls in this principle, since some practices are in general use and yet have proved to be full of risk. Moreover, industries vary and there may not be approved practices in every case.

The obverse of the doctrine of 'care' is the concept of 'negligence' upon which most cases are fought, since it is the alleged absence of care which is said to be the cause of the accident. On the other hand, such a conception implies that the employer is at fault or is to blame – that he is a wrongdoer; in fact he is someone who ought to be dealt with by the criminal law and punished for his actions. In many cases this is precisely what happens, but this is a different matter from the notion of negligence for which he may be summoned by his employee. Negligence in the modern context implies the test of 'reasonable foreseeability',[6] a 'vague, capricious and subjective' standard when applied to the complex situations that arise in modern industry. However, it has been held to contain three elements, all of which must be present.

(*a*) That the situation is one involving the legal duty to take care for the safety of others. Long usage has covered most actions, though new situations arise from time to time that need to be thrashed out in the courts.

(*b*) That conduct in breach of this duty has occurred and can be regarded as negligent.

(*c*) That injury or damage to another person has actually been caused by this conduct.

Certain court decisions have refined these elements still further, and have established the principle that the claim will only succeed if there is a close and direct relationship between the defendant and the plaintiff, as in master and servant, occupier and visitor. And further, that the defendant should have been able to *foresee* the *likelihood* of injury. 'Foreseeability' has already been considered, though its importance lies in the employer himself, the something which he was able to do, or should have been able to do. 'Likelihood' on the other hand, arises out of the set of circumstances, the something which the onlooker would have been able to appreciate. Because it is an objective test, it has been more readily acceptable in the courts as the standard by which the unsafe act might be judged. And as the onus of proof lies with the plaintiff, he is on surer grounds when he stresses this aspect of care.

The law has been further refined in the case of the employer–employee relationship to mean not only the personal care of the employer not to injure his workman, such as the driving of a vehicle by the master in such a way that the worker is hurt, but also his duty (*a*) to provide a safe and healthy place of work with safe plant and machinery, (*b*) to ensure that the method and conduct of the work itself is safe and (*c*) that the staff as a whole are competent and not likely to cause danger, because they were wrongly selected for a job they were unable to do.

Some of these requirements have now been incorporated in employers' statutory duties, but statutory duties vary from industry to industry, while common law ones are the same for all, and cover shops and offices which, for the years under review, did not share the provisions of the Factories Acts.

Safe Place of Work

Much case law has been built round these requirements. For instance, the duty to provide a safe place of work has been decided as meaning that the place should be either occupied by the employer, or under his control. Thus, if a man were sent on a message to the factory next door and was there injured by an improperly placed object, the liability of negligence could not under ordinary circumstances be laid at the door of his own master, unless it could be proved he knew of it or could have foreseen it. But, on his own premises, the employer is obliged to ensure that the plant and other environmental factors are 'reasonably fit for the purpose for which they are used'.[7] He is not, however, liable for 'latent defects not discernible by the exercise of reasonable care and skill', though he is liable, if those defects could have been detected had skill and care been exercised. This general duty of care towards employees has been extended to visitors (Occupiers Liability Act, 1957), that is, to those whom the occupier of the premises has allowed to enter (this excludes trespassers), and he is obliged to see that premises are reasonably safe 'for the purpose for which the visitor or licensee has been invited or permitted'.[8]

As for the provision of safe plant and appliances, there is no duty on the employer to install all the latest safety devices and improvements; but if he is informed of defects, or if he ought to have been aware of them by using reasonable skill and care, he must take immediate steps to remedy them, and would be deemed negligent if he did not.

Safe System of Working

'Safe system of working' is a more difficult conception, and can only be interpreted in the light of the actual circumstances in each factory. Thus, though in general it is taken to include the 'general planning and organization of work, as distinct from the provision, upkeep and use of tools, appliances and machinery',[9] there can be no precise definition.

The position has been interestingly examined by Mr. T. R. Leighton,[10] L.E.B., F.C.I.I., the senior claims official of the Eagle Insurance Company. He has quoted the case of *Wilsons and Clyde Coal Co. Ltd. vs. English* ([1937] 3 All E.R. 628). The simple facts of the case were that English was injured in the haulage way, because he thought nothing was coming. Actually there was, through no fault of anybody, and he was hurt. The court blamed the mine manager (who was a properly qualified man, as by the

Coal Mines Act 1911 he had to be), because his time-table was faulty. The case went to the House of Lords, who had two questions to decide:

1. Granted that the employer is bound by law to provide a safe system of work for his servants, is this obligation satisfied by entrusting the task to a person whom the employer may reasonably deem to be competent – even more competent than the employer? To this the answer given was 'No'.
2. Was the coal company excused further responsibility because it was obliged to appoint a trained official in accordance with the Coal Mines Act? The answer was again 'No'.

Mr. Leighton was particularly impressed by the report, not so much for its content, as for the able review of employers' liability given by the judges, notably Lord Thankerton and Lord Wright, and the Lord President of the High Court, who said: 'There are certain duties owed by a master to his servant, so imperative and so vital to safety, that the master cannot divest himself of responsibility by entrusting their performance to others, so as to avoid liability, in the event of injury arising to the servant, through the neglect of any of these duties'. He went on to describe these duties as the provision of competent staff, adequate material, a proper system, and supervision. This was not put forward as new law, simply the re-stating of old principles. Nor did it cause any ripple in legal and insurance circles at the time. But, Leighton remarks, from that date accident claims have increased in volume, and they have increased because of the issues underlined in the judgment.

There was, for instance, the plea of a 'defective system'. This was nothing new, it had been understood for a hundred years (1839). There was no question of the plea of 'common employment' being advanced, a plea already hedged round with modifications and becoming increasingly unpopular. Instead, the company was found at fault because of its own breach of duty, not through any negligence of the mine manager. The judgment did, however, indicate more clearly what was meant by a 'proper system of working', and said that it meant being subject to proper control, training and discipline. It also meant that an employer was responsible for the lay-out of a job.

This issue was further clarified in 1950 by Lord Oaksey in the *Winter vs. Cardiff* case,[11] when he declared 'where the mode of operation is complicated, or highly dangerous, or prolonged, or involves a number of men performing difficult functions, it is naturally a matter for the employer to take the responsibility of deciding what system shall be adopted. On the other hand where the operation is simple, and the decision how it shall be done has to be taken frequently, it is natural and reasonable that it should be left to the foreman or workman on the spot.'

Competent personnel

The common law duty to employ suitably qualified fellow servants has, in the past, been the one arousing more contention in the courts than any other. It is now alleged that it has little relevance, since the Law Reform (Personal Injuries) Act, 1948, has abolished the defence of 'common employment', and employers are responsible for the negligence of their staff, whether competent or not. Further, this general duty has to be shouldered even if the employer has delegated the work to independent contractors, though the 'casual negligence of independent contractors' would not be his.[12]

Against all these accusations several well-tried defences have developed. Rowntree[13] has classified them into four categories:

(*a*) *That the accident was inevitable.* This has been taken to mean that it happened notwithstanding the exercise of reasonable care and diligence by all concerned. Thus, an event can occur outside human control and foresight, an Act of God, like an earthquake or storm. Or it may be the result of an emergency, in which the defendant acted reasonably in view of the position in which he found himself, as when an animal goes out of control and injures the workman, in spite of every effort by his master to avoid damage.

(*b*) *That the injured person was a trespasser.* We have seen how legislation in 1957 (Occupiers Liability Act) has replaced a mass of case law on this, and has safeguarded the interests of visitors and licensees to a limited degree, but not of trespassers.

(*c*) *That the servant was acting outside the scope of his authority.* If an employer can prove that the worker was disobeying express instructions, and was acting contrary to the employer's interests, the defence might be accepted. For instance, if a clerk broke open the employer's safe to steal the money and suffered injury, he would have no case against the employer. But if a worker, contrary to the express instructions of his master, opened the fencing surrounding an engine in order to mend the engine while it was in motion, and in so doing caught his clothing on a moving part and was injured, the employer would not be able to claim disobedience as a defence, since the action of the worker was in the employer's interests. (The employer might be charged in the Criminal Courts for allowing the accident to happen.)

(*d*) *Contributory negligence* is closely allied to disobedience, and has been the subject of much litigation and will probably continue to be so. Prior to the Law Reform (Contributory Negligence) Act 1945, an employer could claim contributory negligence on the part of the plaintiff and win his case. It was even possible to do so if the case were a breach of statutory duty (this was decided in 1940). Thus when a case was submitted, the court had to sort out the various causes of the accident and decide which were the most important. On this basis they then had to decide who had been responsible for the important causes. If it could be shown the employer was mainly to blame, then he would be obliged to pay damages, but if it were the worker, then the case was dismissed. It was all or nothing. Since 1945, the court has been allowed to take all causes into consideration and apportion the blame between the parties. This apportionment then becomes the basis of the damages. Thus the total damages relating to the injury are computed, and the employer has to pay that proportion of the total damages which his responsibility is said to bear to the accident itself.[14]

Mr. Justice Stable, commenting on a case at Lincolnshire Assizes on 10 December, 1959, said:[15] 'I have never quite understood the basis of this particular doctrine.' He then proceeded to postulate the duty a man owes to himself and his family, not to take unnecessary risks, a duty an 'employer cannot regard as being a duty to him', and the duty a man has 'to further the interests of his employers'. If, in the pursuance of the employer's interests he acts foolishly, or takes unjustifiable risks in an excess of zeal, or in a moment of absentmindedness, or inadvertence, or carelessness, can there be a finding of contributory negligence? Mr. Justice Stable thought not, provided that the injured man was not playing the fool, or indulging in some activity wholly outside his job.

REFERENCES

1. A. Wilson & H. Levy, *Workmen's Compensation.* 2 Vols. (Oxford U.P., 1939.) Vol. 1, p. 5.
2. J. Munkman, *Employers' Liability at Common Law.* (Butterworth, 1959.) p. 1.
3. Ibid. p. 68.
4. H. Rowntree, *Common Law Liability.* (Buckley, 1951.) pp. 185–6.
5. Munkman, op. cit. p. 32.
6. Ibid. p. 23.
7. Rowntree, op. cit. p. 188.
8. Munkman, op. cit. p. 152.
9. Rowntree, op. cit. p. 191.
10. *Journal of Chartered Insurance Institute* 1953. Vol. 50.
11. *Winter vs. Cardiff R.D.C.* [1950] 1 All E.R. 819.
12. Munkman, op. cit. p. 80.
13. Rowntree, op. cit. Cap XIII.
14. Munkman, op. cit. p. 444.
15. *The Times*, 11.12.1959.

10

STATUTORY DUTIES

IN the relationships between worker and employer, the latter has gathered, through the years, a number of duties which are statutorily defined and which he is obliged to honour. If he does not, the worker can sue him for damages. The right of the worker so to sue was not granted by the first Factory Act in 1802, where action was limited to the criminal courts. But, by 1844, Factory Acts had begun to take on their modern form, their provisions including the necessity to fence machinery, and from this time forward the worker was not precluded from seeking damages by civil action.

The general principles upon which a worker can prove a breach of statutory duty would seem to be [1] (*a*) that the statute imposes upon the defendant a duty which is intended to protect the plaintiff against harm of some kind, (*b*) that the defendant has failed to perform his duty, (*c*) that this breach of duty has resulted in harm to the plaintiff, which is of the kind contemplated by the statute. Thus, the most important requirement is that the breach should have caused the injury complained of. This is often very difficult, as the case of *Bonnington Castings Ltd. v. Wardlaw* (1956) illustrates.[2] In this case the worker had contracted silicosis from breathing dust at work. It was shown that he had breathed two kinds of dust, one that should have been extracted at source, and another. The plea nearly failed because it could not be proved that the particular dust, which should have been extracted, and where the employer was in breach of his statutory duty, was the one that caused the silicosis. The plea only succeeded because this dust 'materially contributed' to the condition.*

* Munkman, op. cit. says (p. 162) that 'it is not correct to say that negligence and breach of statutory duty are one and the same thing – though in Scotland they appear to be'.

The term an 'absolute duty' is commonly used to describe statutory duties. This always means that what the statute prescribes must be strictly performed. Thus there is an absolute duty to fence a machine if it is dangerous, even if the danger could only arise out of the disobedience or neglect of an employee. On the other hand the employer is not expected to guard against dangers that no one could be expected to foresee, and the 1937 Factory Act leaves the matter fluid in certain instances by using the words 'practicable' and 'reasonable'. So there is sometimes room for argument even in interpreting what is prescribed by the statute.[3] The word 'absolute' also implies that the statute requires a certain result, and it is a breach if this result is not obtained, even though the person liable to perform the duty has done everything within his power. Thus the question of negligence does not arise. A third meaning attached to 'absolute duty' is that it cannot be delegated. There is room for difference of opinion on this point if the plaintiff is himself an expert and should have seen that the danger was excluded.

It is generally contended that statutory duties are more 'absolute' in their obligations than common law, though, as we have seen, the question of what is 'reasonably practicable' may arise in either case.

Thus one source of defence in breach of statutory duty cases may be 'practicability'.[4] Where the law is vague (e.g. Section 25 of the Factory Act, 1937, imposes the duty to keep a means of access safe 'so far as is reasonably practicable') the court has to decide what is feasible, taking all the circumstances into consideration. But the only other defence is to deny the obligation. This may mean that there was no duty that the defendant had to obey, or that, accepting the existence of a duty, it had not been broken, or that the plaintiff himself was not within the benefit of the statute, or that the accident was something quite different from what the statute was designed to prevent. Of course 'contributory negligence' may be put forward as well, but this would be an acceptance of responsibility by the employer, though only partial. The question of 'the right of indemnity' against the manufacturer who supplied the machine or material which proved dangerous, is another argument that is often used, though it cannot absolve the employer from breach of duty.

REFERENCES

1. Munkman, op. cit. p. 163.
2. Ibid. p. 164.
3. Ibid. p. 172.
4. Ibid. p. 178.

11

REJECTED THEORIES

IT has been suggested that, whereas in the early nineteenth century case law operated against the interests of the worker, modern case law, especially in the House of Lords, has tended to favour him. Consequently many theories, which were invoked in defence of the employer in the past, were gradually whittled away by case law, until they were abandoned altogether by Act of Parliament. The most common of these theories were:

(*a*) *Common employment.* This dates from a test case in 1837 (*Priestley v. Fowler*) in which an employer would not be required to accept responsibility for the injury to a workman, if the accident had occurred as a result of the negligence of another employee. The argument used to be valid that, when a workman entered the service of his employer, he implicitly accepted the risk of injury from the acts of his fellow workmen, and provided the employer could show he had used reasonable care in selecting his workmen, he was not required to bear the responsibility for any negligence they might have shown. The Employers' Liability Act of 1880 was the first breach in this doctrine, because under it a worker could successfully claim damages from defects in 'ways, works machinery, or plant, or from the negligence of some person placed in a position of superintendence, or whose orders the worker had to obey'. The Act was not as effective in providing damages to the injured worker as had been expected, because it was always open to the employer to plead 'contributory negligence' by the injured man, or that he had acted outside his authority, or that he had wilfully committed an act which had led to the accident. The relative ineffectiveness of the Act led directly to the first workmen's compensation legislation. Meanwhile, the theory of 'common employment' continued, though its effectiveness as a defence by employers gradually grew less, and cases fought on it increasingly failed to succeed, e.g. in 1939 in *Radcliffe v. Ribble Motor Services Ltd.*,[1] where two drivers were involved in the same accident, the House of Lords rejected the defence of common employment, on the grounds that the risk of injury by a vehicle driven by a fellow servant was not one of the peculiar 'risks and perils incidental to the performance of a worker's service'. Finally, towards the end of the Second World War, in 1944, the Home Secretary appointed a committee on 'alternative remedies' under the chairmanship of Sir Walter Monckton.[2] The committee argued that it is false to say a worker accepts as part of his employment the risk of being injured by his fellow workman's negligence. The results of applying the doctrine are often illogical, they declared, since it depended on whether a fellow worker was employed by the same employer or not. As a result of the committee's recommendations the Law Reform (Personal Injuries) Act, 1948, was passed, abolishing the doctrine of common employment altogether, and forbidding private agreements including it. Thus ended a theory that had lasted more than 100 years, and its going hardly caused a ripple, so much had its functioning been limited in latter years by case law.

(*b*) *The principle of 'volenti non fit injuria'*. This implies that when a workman accepts wages, he makes a 'contract of labour', and accepts responsibility for the normal risks of his employment. In the nineteenth century this was an important theory, and was used effectively in the courts to limit an employer's liability. It had two branches. On the one hand, it was said that if a worker consented to an act which in the event resulted in injury to him, he could not afterwards complain of it as a legal wrong. Or, if a worker freely and voluntarily agreed to incur a risk, and injury materialized, he could not claim damages. The development of statutory duties on the employer severely limited the scope of this argument, since it could never be advanced as a defence in a case involving these duties. And the progressive acceptance by the courts that an employer had a special relationship to his workers, which put them in a more favourable position when his duty to exercise care was concerned, has made the theory unacceptable even when cases are not fought on breaches of statutory duty. Hence, while the defence may be raised as part of 'contributory negligence' it has little effect on its own account in modern trials.

(*c*) *Delegation* used to be a defence, because, if an employer could show that he had employed a skilled and competent man to perform the duty, then it was this man's fault if it was not performed, and a workman was injured. This was early rebutted, particularly in the Employers' Liability Act, 1880, and the defence is now obsolete. However, the question is raised as to what are the rights the skilled and competent man himself may have if he should be injured because of his own negligence. If it is a breach of statutory duty, there can be no delegation of responsibility for the duty, and any breach can be tried in the criminal courts. On the other hand, if the plaintiff is the sole cause of his injuries, the maxim 'no man can profit by his own wrong' should operate.[3] So the skilled and competent man injured solely by his own negligence in an area where the employer has no statutory duty to exercise care would not be able to sue the employer for damages. In this limited sphere, delegation would appear still to be a valid defence.

(*d*) *Election.* Until 1948, the doctrine of 'election' operated, because according to the Workmen's Compensation Act 1925 (sect. 29) if a worker had claims under both the Workmen's Compensation Acts and the common law, he had to choose which claim to pursue; he could not gain from both. The position was severely criticized as putting the worker in an intolerable situation as he had to estimate his chances. If there was a strong element of contributory negligence, he would have to rely on workmen's compensation, but if he thought he could get a larger sum if he sued his employer, he might choose that method, with all its disadvantages of exacerbation of feeling between himself and his employer, the long wait for the case to be completed, and the gamble that the case might not succeed. Beveridge regretted the 'election' principle, because[4] 'the needs of the injured person should be met at once', and election prevented this, since any 'alternative remedy' was bound to take some time to test. The insurance companies, meanwhile, were aware of the odium in which they stood because of this. And, early in the Second World War, they made an agreement with the Home Office that, pending the revision of workmen's compensation legislation, they would not apply the doctrine of election harshly. If a worker applied for workers' compensation and, within three months of the accident, filed a case for damages under common law, the company would not then refuse compensation, because the alternative remedy was being tried, but would continue to pay until the case was heard.[5] This might be considered generosity on the part of the insurance companies, were it not for their proviso that compensation in such cases depended on the worker fighting his own case. If he consulted a legal adviser, or an official of a trade union or an approved society, the offer lapsed. Since few cases are so difficult as these, it is hard to understand how a worker could expect to make a reasonable choice unless he took advice.

Investigating the whole question of 'election' was one of the chief functions of the Monckton Committee on 'alternative remedies' (1944–6). They were charged to inquire how far the recovery of damages, in respect of personal injury, should be affected by the new proposals for social insurance. Thus, when the two Law Reform Acts were passed (1945 and 1948) giving legislative sanction to some of the Monckton Committee recommendations, among the most important provisions were the abolition of the theory of common employment, and the rejection of the doctrine of election. A person injured after July 1948 could receive both the appropriate national insurance benefit and damages, though henceforth the amount awarded in damages would take into account any cash benefit already received – up to a maximum of 50 per cent for five years – and any contributory negligence. Medical benefit obtained and paid for outside the national health scheme, on the other hand, would be allowable in damages. A time limit was also instituted and no application would be valid beyond three years after the date on which the cause of action accrued.*

(*e*) *Contracting out* was a well-tried safeguard by employers, who wished to minimize the risk of having civil cases brought

* June 1959 the Queen's Bench ruled this to mean the date when the employer was last in breach.

against them by injured workers. The 1880 Employers' Liability Act, it was said, had been reduced to negligible proportions by workers agreeing, as part of their contract, to refrain from seeking damages should they be injured. Only by making it unlawful to contract out of the Workers' Compensation Acts did they become the reasonably satisfactory schemes they proved to be. The practice, however, has continued in a limited form down to more recent times. In 1948, for instance, one more loophole was abolished by the Law Reform Act. This made it illegal for an employer to make a separate contract with an employee, absolving himself from the consequences of negligence by a fellow worker (the doctrine of common employment). How far contracting-out of civil damages for injury still plays any part in the relations between master and servant is hard to tell. The absence of strong representations from the trade unions would suggest the danger is slight.

REFERENCES

1. Dinsdale, *History of Accident Insurance in Great Britain.* (Stone & Cox, 1954.) Cap XIII.
2. *Alternative Remedies.* Cttee. (Monckton, Ch.) Reports; 1944–5 Cmd. 6580, Cmd. 6642, vi.
3. Munkman, op. cit. p. 460.
4. *Social Insurances & Allied Services.* Inter-Dept. Cttee. (Beveridge, Ch.) Report, para. 259. 1942–3 Cmd. 6404, vi.
5. Dinsdale, op. cit. p. 161.

12

THE GENERAL POSITION SINCE 1948—A SOCIAL ASSESSMENT

NO statistical evidence is available to give point to any detailed examination of the civil damages position since the great changes of 1948. Even the published returns of insurance companies are no help. For employers' liability business, separately compiled until 1947, has, in most cases, been incorporated in the general title 'miscellaneous accident', and includes all kinds of accidents (except motor and personal ones).

In spite of the absence of firm information, several important issues have been raised since 1948 about the use of the ancient right to sue those responsible, if injury has been suffered. Of these issues three may be selected as of outstanding interest:

(*a*) the purpose of damages in a modern industrialized society,

(*b*) the problem of diminution of damages,

(*c*) the alleged increase in the number of cases brought to court.

(*a*) *The Purpose of Damages*

Much has been said by learned judges in the courts and written by legal academics about the general principles concerning the purpose of damages in common law, and about the rules which ought to govern the actual damages levied. But the quest for some scientific statement still continues. There seems to be general agreement that the principle of *restitutio in integrum* is the main consideration. As Lord Blackburn said in 1880,[1] 'Where any injury is to be compensated by damages, in settling the sum of money to be given for reparation of damages, you should as nearly as possible get at that sum of money which will put the party who has been injured, or who has suffered, in the same position as he would have been in, if he had not sustained the wrong for which he is now getting his compensation or reparation.' It is not the intention of this study to argue the implications of this dictum, which has guided the courts ever since, nor to consider whether pain and suffering can have a monetary value, or whether humiliation and loss of face enter into a negligence charge. What is of concern in a review of general policy is to look at the position as a whole.

For in a civil case of this kind there are at least two parties involved: the workman whose injury has to be compensated, and who is obliged to prove negligence or other approved fault by his master; and the employer, who, if the case is proved, has to pay. The effect of the law on the employer is as important as on the worker. If he has committed a criminal act, as in certain breaches of his statutory duty, he may be prosecuted in the criminal courts where a maximum sentence is known and may be given. This would clearly be regarded as a punishment for him, and the worker would gain nothing from it. Punishment, however, in its modern connotation has in it several elements. It may be concerned with retribution, in which society expresses its disapproval of a convicted employer and tries to hurt him either through his pocket or, in flagrant cases, by sending him to prison. Or it may wish to deter him from such action in the future. Or it may hope to prevent others from similar negligence by the knowledge that punitive action will be taken. Sentences therefore vary considerably, having regard to which aspect of punishment is uppermost in the minds of the court, and the kind of treatment that the court thinks will achieve the object they have in mind. But their room for manœuvre is severely limited, as criminal law sets maxima to the sentences available for each criminal act.

Whether or not an employer is dealt with by criminal law is immaterial to the right of the worker to sue him for compensation, or to the right of the civil court to express its disapproval of him (even though no case may have been brought against him in the criminal courts). Through the device of 'exemplary damages' it can add to the compensation for the wrong sustained by the worker an additional amount by way of punishment to the employer. This development has been recognized in law since the middle of the eighteenth century (1763) when Pratt, L.C.J., stated in *Wilkes v. Wood*,[2] 'Damages are designed not solely as a satisfaction to the injured person, but likewise as a punishment for the guilty, to deter from any such proceedings for the future, and as a proof of the detestation of the jury to the action itself.' The principle has been endorsed many times since then, and in civil cases of tort (though not as a rule in contract) the court can take upon itself the double function of awarding restitution to the worker and of punishing the employer, with all the nuances that the word in modern times has come to contain.*

How far punishment of this kind has any deterrent value no one knows. Professor Glanville Williams thought it had, when he stated publicly (*Listener*, 6 December, 1956) that 'heavier damages for negligence have the effect of causing employers to look to their safety precautions, and consider whether they can be improved'. The nineteenth-century trade unionists thought so too, when they encouraged their members to sue negligent employers as a means of improving the safety of the mine or the workshop (see Part I, page 39). That the validity of the assumption is open to doubt is expressed by Mr. J. L. Williams in his challenging book.[3] 'In the last thirty years,' he said, 'the accident rates have not declined to any significant extent, although there has been a noticeable increase in damages claims. On this basis, the most that can be said in favour of the deterrent theory is that there might have been many more accidents but for damages claims.' Further, a prudent employer can always protect himself against civil litigation by the simple device of insurance. 'On the payment of a definite annual premium to an ordinary insurance company, he is indemnified against any loss by claims under the Act; the company, to boot, taking all the trouble off his hands. The fear of damages may here and there induce a small master to obey more promptly than before the factory inspector's order to guard a driving wheel, or fence a lift shaft. But in the great staple industries, insurance against accidents at a rate of premium which is, in practice, uniform for all the firms in the trade, is

* The arguments for and against 'exemplary damages' may be found on pp. 34–36, Professor Street. *Principles of the Law of Damages*, op. cit.

becoming almost as much a matter of course as insurance against fire.' Beveridge, in his famous report, says much the same thing. For, as he showed, in all the years of workmen's compensation, when the employer was directly responsible for cash benefit to his injured workers, the fact that his pocket was being hit seemed to have no more effect on his concern for safety than he would have felt in any case. Safety has developed from other motives and has been stimulated from other sources.

Whether or not 'exemplary damages' do anything more than satisfy an urge for revenge felt by the victims (thus preventing them taking their own vengeance), the question may well be asked whether the plaintiff should be at the receiving end of an action resulting in them. Professor Street has pointed out that the distinction between 'aggravated damages' (compensation for hurt feelings, etc.) and 'exemplary' ones is sometimes difficult to make; it might be said that, because an employer has been grossly negligent, the plaintiff's injury is made all the worse in his own mind by the knowledge that it need not have happened at all. This is an understandable state of affairs, and there seems no reason why damages should not be adjusted accordingly. But so long as all his loss has fairly and equitably been taken into account in the quantum of damages, there seems no justification for him to receive more because the employer is being punished. It would seem more logical to transfer the punitive element of damages to the criminal courts, where fines accrue to the community.

(*b*) *The Problem of Diminution of Damages*

Up to 1948, when the doctrine of 'election' was ended, an injured worker could elect to take workmen's compensation cash benefit from his employer, or ask him to pay damages under common law. In either case the employer (or his insurance company) had to pay, and there was some justice in not requiring him to pay twice. Very often, if it seemed likely that the worker would elect to go to common law, the case would be settled out of court; and the damages decided upon became a compromise between what the court might have awarded and what the workmen's compensation would have cost.

On the face of it this system no longer pertains, since an industrially injured person is assured of his national injuries benefit, whether he claims damages or not. If, on the other hand, he decides to claim damages, the question then is, should he benefit from both the full compensation and the state insurance.

In 1944 the problem was referred to the Monckton Committee on 'alternative remedies', who considered it very carefully, and decided by a majority to accept Beveridge's ruling that[4] 'no injured person should have the same need met twice'. Of the many arguments they used, two seemed to have influenced them most. The first was that an injured man had certain needs (medical and personal), and that so long as these needs were met, he should not receive anything further. And the second was that so long as a person, through his ordinary thrift and foresight, provided something more than he needed, he should be allowed to benefit, but that state insurance was not in this category. It was a compulsory payment made because of his status as an employed person, and not by voluntary saving. Therefore, in any consideration of what he received, his own private thrift should be ignored, but his national insurance should not. Certain members of the committee (notably Mr. W. P. Allen and Mr. Luke Fawcett and, in a different way, Mr. F. W. Beney) opposed the arguments and the conclusions reached by the rest of the committee, and accordingly signed minority reports.

The passage of time has not strengthened the force of the majority decision, based as it was on too close an adherence to the Beveridge recommendations (though not to his arguments, since he did not discuss the question at all), and too little appreciation of the entirely new relationship on these matters between employers and workers, which the new National Insurance (Industrial Injuries) Act was about to inaugurate, Thus, whereas the employer used to be solely responsible for the compensation to his own injured workmen and, in theory, was therefore put to greater expense the greater the injury, he is now a compulsory contributor, along with all other employers and workers, to an industrial injuries fund, out of which payments are made to the injured workman. He is no longer personally responsible for his own workers, and is obliged to contribute whether his worker is injured or not. It might be said that there is no difference from his practice heretofore, when he voluntarily insured against his personal liability. But ordinary people would see a great difference between a personal liability to compensate, and a compulsory obligation to pay into a fund. The difference is enlarged by the altered status of the worker, who, under earlier legislation, received benefit from the man he knew as his employer, but who subsequently became a compulsory contributor in his own right, and therefore the recipient of benefit towards which he had paid as much as his mastsr. The responsibility of the employer to his workmen has become less personal and, in this sense, less real than before.

Consequently, should the worker win an action against his master for damages in common law, he does so on an entirely separate issue from his own receipt of injuries benefit. He wins his case on the breach of the law, but he receives his benefit because he has been incapacitated. There seems no reason to confuse the issues. And, since the employer is no longer personally responsible for the injured man's weekly benefit, there is no justification for any relief in the total of damages levied against him. Furthermore, though it is not the purpose of this essay to encourage the continuation of the principle of exemplary damages, so long as punishment remains an element in the award of damages, it is wholly unjustifiable that an employer's pocket should be saved because there happens to be a system of state insurance.

The Monckton Committee was concerned less with the employers' angle than with the workers'. If, as they seemed to assume, damages were concerned solely with restitution to the worker of any loss he might have sustained, there was no case for having the loss met more than once. Yet, in law, the principle was accepted as early as 1874 in the case of *Bradburn v. the Great Western Railway*,[5] when it was held that a sum received by the plaintiff, in respect of an accident insurance policy, could not be applied in reduction of the damages awarded to him for his personal injuries. It was then stated that he did not receive his insurance money 'because of the accident, but because he had made a contract providing for the contingency; an accident must occur to entitle him to it, but it was not the accident but his contract which was the cause of his receiving it'. The Monckton Committee argued that a private insurance and a compulsory one were entirely different, and that the Bradburn case did not apply. There has been no opportunity to test this in the courts since the law has enacted (Law Reform (Personal Injuries) Act, 1948) that injuries benefit shall reduce the amount of the damages. But the rationale for such a situation is not easy to distinguish. It would seem more reasonable to suggest that civil law damages are a private matter between the employer and the worker and that, provided there is no question of contributory negligence, a worker is entitled to receive from his employer the total amount of his loss under the headings allowed by the law, as he would do if his alternative financial resources were private means, or his Friendly Society benefit.

One other aspect of the matter has also been widely discussed, and that is the proposal to repay to the industrial injuries fund, in whole or in part, the cash benefit paid out by them to the worker, if the worker has obtained compensation through damages. Apart from the expense and difficulty of administering such a proposal, a matter of principle is involved. It has been the strength of the national insurances that no means test is applied, so that the rich may draw benefit equally with the poor, and the man who is receiving his full salary equally with the one whose employer pays him nothing. There would be little to commend it if the rule should be broken for damages cases alone. Whether damages should be taxed is a different question, and it might well be that the receipt of capital sums may attract taxation. If this were a general policy, not singling out damages for special treatment, there might be something to be said in its favour.

When the Law Reform (Personal Injuries) Bill came to be discussed, the Labour government, apparently in some embarrassment, accepted a compromise, and while refusing to introduce the Monckton Committee recommendation that no injured worker should receive more from insurance benefit and damages together than he would have received from one source (the larger) alone, they could not ignore the Beveridge argument. Thus it was enacted that damages should be assessed according to the usual rules, and from the total should be deducted half of the value of any industrial injury or disablement benefit or sickness benefit the plaintiff might have received, or which might accrue during the five years after the accident. Many difficulties of interpretation have already appeared from this wholly unjustifiable clause.

(c) Rise in the Number of Cases

In spite of the absence of verifiable data, it has been widely and persistently stated that there was a brisk increase in the number of common law cases brought during the years after 1948. There were even suggestions that workers were at fault in this, and that many were suffering from 'compensationitis'. The reasons alleged in the Press and elsewhere were, the abolition of the system of 'election' in 1948, the introduction of the legal aid scheme two years later and, mainly, the growth in strength and assertiveness of the trade unions, who were said to have encouraged an undue number of their members to begin an action in the courts.

The belief is too widespread to be discussed without some examination of what evidence there is: the trade unions themselves have not sought to deny the growth in the number of claims for damages, nor that there has been acceleration since 1948, as the climate for such an advance in their members' interests has become more favourable. But it is no new thing. Mr. J. L. Williams LL.B. of the Labour Research Department has claimed that[6] 'after the 1914–18 war there was a steady increase in cases involving safety, and the number increased very considerably from 1930 onwards', and that this was a direct result of stronger trade union organization providing legal assistance for injured members. Dr. Dinsdale,[7] director of education in the Chartered Insurance Institute, on the other hand, would place the moment of change at 1937, with the passing of the Factories Act. This Act substantially increased the number and scope of statutory duties, making breaches a more common occurrence, and consequently increasing the risk of actions for damages.

The evidence becomes a little more factual[8] when one examines the statements made to the Beveridge Committee at the beginning of the war. The Accident Offices Association, and the Mutual Insurance Companies Association (embracing the main insurance offices operating employers' liability policies) stated, that of all the workers' compensation applications that were made in the years 1935–7 (about half a million), rather fewer than 0·1 per cent gave rise to claims for damages (about 500). However, it was also suggested in evidence (Question 7594) that the proportion of cases which began with the possibility of a common law claim was higher than this.

The contention that claims increased after the passing of the

1937 Factories Act, and in spite of the system of 'election', is supported to some extent by figures supplied by the Mutual Insurance Companies Association to the Beveridge Committee. For, in the years 1939, 1940 and 1941, the percentage of common law claims to workers' compensation claims handled by their members was 0·17, 0·32 and 0·26 respectively. Compared with an average of 0·1 per cent before 1937, there was a small increase. But as the total number of common law claims (a few hundred each year) was small compared with the number of workers' compensation claims, the situation had not assumed very much importance. Whether the percentage has radically altered since 1948 it would be interesting to know. The Insurance Directory and Year Book, giving figures about employers' liability for twenty-two companies in 1951, showed that seven had registered an increase in claims since 1948, and fifteen a decrease. But, as only a small minority of companies were showing their employers' liability business separately, it would be false to assume from them that a fall in claims was the general experience in the insurance world.

On the contrary, Mr. T. W. O. Coleman, the home accident manager of the Norwich Union Fire Insurance Society, addressing his fellow members of the Chartered Insurance Institute in 1954[9] suggested that, whereas the period from 1948–9 was relatively quiet, between 1950–53 claims under 'employers' liability' rose rapidly in incidence and amount, and as it was a period of financial inflation the costs and damages in such actions rose too.

Another piece of evidence may be obtained from the volumes of the All England Law Reports, which describe cases of legal difficulty or significance that have been decided in the High Courts of England. The list is merely a selection of all the cases that are tried each year, and does not touch the vast majority which begin and end in the lower courts or are settled out of court. If, however, it may be presumed that on the average the proportion of cases that reaches the higher courts is approximately the same, taking one year with another, then any significant increase in the number of cases reported in the All England Law Reports would indicate a corresponding increase in the total number of cases tried in all the courts and of those which do not reach the court. The figures for the period after 1948 were:

1949 = 16		
1950 = 9		
1951 = 8		
1952 = 20		
1953 = 25	Ten-year average = 21·6	
1954 = 24		
1955 = 37		
1956 = 34		
1957 = 23		
1958 = 23		
1959 = 15		
1960 = 15	Four-year average = 14	
1961 = 17		
1962 = 9		

As the ten-year average before 1949 was 9·2, there seems to be some evidence of an increase in the number of civil cases brought by workers after the introduction of the industrial injuries scheme, and the abolition of the system of 'election'. The date of change appears to have been about 1951–52 (by which time the Legal Aid Act was in its stride). On the other hand 1955 was a peak year, and the steady decline thereafter has brought the annual incidence to pre-war proportions (in 1937 there were fourteen cases, and twelve in 1938). So far no convincing reason for the apparent decline in recourse to alternative remedies since 1955 has been advanced, and it may not be permanent.

While it is feasible to think that there has been an increase in the number of actions for damages, the grounds upon which they have been fought have remained as before. Dr. Dinsdale[10] has enumerated them as: personal negligence of the employer; the negligence of fellow servants; the negligence of the employer in the use of reasonable care and skill in the choice of servants; the provision of proper and suitable plant and system of working; his negligence in remedying structural and similar defects; and the breach of statutory duties. It is the general opinion that the abolition of the defence of common employment has made little difference, either to the number of claims on insurance companies, or to the goodwill or otherwise between masters and servants.

On the other hand, it is possible there has been a change in the standards of 'negligence', especially those concerned with statutory duties, because it is said higher requirements, some would say, 'impossibly high' are now demanded. Coleman[11] quotes two cases of this: *Pugh v. Manchester Dry Docks* ([1954] 1 All E.R. 600) where the machinery was held to be inadequately fenced, though, according to Coleman, if the fencing had been adequate the machine would have been unusable; and *Cork v. Kirby Maclean Ltd.* ([1952] 2 All E.R. 402) in which an accident had occurred to an epileptic employee. It was held to be equally the fault of the employer, even though the worker had not disclosed his complaint.

Whether the provision of state-assisted legal aid since 1950 has affected the situation is difficult to say. Legal aid is not free, except to those whose means are very small, and many who might have stood a good chance to win a civil case do not bring one because the cost can be so high, even to the assisted litigants, and the results so much of a gamble as to be not worth the expense. Moreever, the delay and the worry often seem too big a price to pay, unless the case is very strong and there are powerful backers as in some of the trade unions.

Nevertheless, since the way is now open to bring an action while receiving injury benefit, and since the grounds upon which claims can be made increase with each new Factory, Mines or other industrial Act, and at every stage in the build-up of case law, and since the amount of damages awarded can be so substantial, there has clearly been an incentive for the number of claims to grow since 1948. The tendency may have begun at least ten years earlier and, if it has been accelerated since 1948, public comment has been stimulated not so much by the small claims that are settled in or out of court, but by a few large awards of damages that have been made from time to time by the High Court.

REFERENCES

1. H. Street, *Principles of the Law of Damages*. (Sweet & Maxwell, 1962.) p. 3.
2. Ibid. p. 29.
3. J. L. Williams, *Accidents & Ill Health at Work*. (Staples, 1960.) p. 278.
4. *Social Insurance & Allied Services*. op. cit. para. 260. (1942–3 Cmd. 6404, vi.)
5. H. Street, op. cit. p. 74.
6. Williams, op. cit. p. 68.

7. Dinsdale, op. cit. p. 130.
8. *Social Insurance & Allied Services*. Inter-Dept. Cttee. App. G. Memos. of Ev.; Ev.; 1942–3 Cmd. 6405, vi.
9. *Journal of Chartered Insurance Institute* 1956. Vol. 53.
10. Dinsdale. op. cit. Cap. XIII.
11. *Journal of Chartered Insurance Institute*. op. cit.

THE ISSUES

IT would seem that the policy of any humane society should be concerned with the following general principles:

(1) The need to pursue positive safety, that is, not only to prevent accidents and disease but actively to promote safety so that accidents become the exception.

(2) If, due to the waywardness of circumstance, persons are injured or fall ill, there is the need for them to be restored to their former vigour as soon as possible, and with as little pain, worry and inconvenience as may be; nor should their incapacity to earn cause them, and their families, to be the losers financially.

(3) If anyone is at fault, and blame can be brought home to him, it should be the responsibility of society to deal with him, by punishment, by treatment, by depriving him of the opportunity to repeat his fault.

These three would seem to be reasonable aims for any society. When placed against a backcloth of such dimensions, the whole British system of industrial injury insurance and alternative remedies seems very partial and inadequate, and to some degree unjust.

1. *Safety*

It has been tacitly assumed by most writers (and to some extent in this study too) that were a system of compensation directly and financially linked with the number of accidents (or, conversely, the number and quality of safety precautions) there would be a potent and effective incentive to employers to avoid negligence, honour their statutory duties, and pursue an actively safe régime. To assume this is too naïve, because it takes no account of the complexity of modern industrial power, the impotence of financial penalties, or the effectiveness of the insurance system. If it could be taken for granted that all working units were small and were personally conducted by the owner, and that he responded as the mythical 'economic man' would always do if threatened with financial loss, it might be possible to assure the maximum of safety by imposing a heavy penalty whenever an accident occurred. But modern industry is growing larger,* and control becomes more remote as managerial functions are delegated. Thus the seat of the accident may be separated from the seat of ultimate responsibility both by space and by a long chain of persons, roles and functions which go to make the industrial pattern. Clearly, it is the responsibility of the man at the top to make every link in the chain as safety-conscious as himself, but it is idle to believe that this can be achieved simply by imposing financial penalties on him.

Moreover, as industry places so much emphasis on the possibility of increasing production by offering financial incentives to both workers and management, and as some safety precautions, if properly used, will actually slow down output (see Part I, p. 13) there may even be financial rewards in the use of unsafe methods of work. The employer has therefore to choose between a form of payment which tacitly encourages workers to break the law, but which brings greater prosperity to the business in higher output, and the danger of accidents which may bring their own financial penalties. In any case, recourse to insurance will blur the sharpest impact of any system of financial levies on accidents, levies which could not be imposed justly since some industries, like mining, are by their very nature more liable to accidents than others, and are not always controllable by man but by nature itself.

The problem of safety, in whatever sphere, is a major one, and is being tackled by education, persuasion, propaganda, research and in the last resort by force. Yet its solution remains elusive, and it would be folly to think the financial motive would succeed where all else does not. Unless and until the problem is mastered, the other issues remain to plague us by their difficulties.

2. *Benefit*

Society has already accepted the proposition that when a person is unable to earn he should be helped, so the real question to be faced is whether he should be a privileged beneficiary because his sickness arose out of his work, or whether this division into

* In 1935 the percentage of workers employed in establishments of 1,000 employees and over was 21·4, in 1959 it was 33·6 (Annual Abstract of Stats. No. 84, 1935–46. *Min. of Labour Gazette*, Dec. 1959).

industrial and non-industrial ill-health has grown to be artificial in modern society.

Attempts have been made to examine the issue in Part II (p. 90) and, while it is agreed that history is very much on the side of a special scheme, it is difficult to find much weight in the remaining arguments. Were this view to be generally accepted, some might claim that the only logical course would be to abolish forthwith the whole of the industrial injuries insurance scheme. But logic is not always the wisest counsellor in human affairs. For it is sometimes reasonable to keep an illogical detail so that a wider aim may be achieved.

It was suggested earlier that the ultimate aim of any democratic society should be to help those incapable of work from becoming financial losers. This means that society's purpose should not be the provision of a mere guaranteed basic minimum, as the national insurance scheme does for the sick (with a higher scale for the work-injured), or even benefit graded according to contributions, as the Labour Party plan of 1963 has suggested, but a competence equal to what would have been available had no illness supervened. This is no new idea, since it has been recognized as the very foundation of damages assessment under the common law. What undermines the reasonableness of the present position is the part that chance plays in its administration. If a man breaks his leg before he enters the factory gate, other things being equal, he will receive sickness benefit calculated on his minimum requirements while he is away from work. If he breaks his leg within the factory precincts, other things being equal, he will have the right to injury benefit at a rate above the minimum, and may also be able to sue his employer for negligence, thus receiving damages enough to cover all his financial loss. From the employer's point of view too the position is hardly satisfactory. In both cases he temporarily loses the services of one of his men. But in the one case he must be aware that his employee is ill-provided for, and in the other that he himself is liable to undergo the worry and expense of a court case to establish negligence and award damages. Of course, many employers develop 'fringe benefits' to take care of the temporary absence of their workers, and doubtless the payment of full wages during increasingly long periods of incapacity will extend throughout industry, thus partly solving the problem of how to deal with financial loss. Yet, in the best planned schemes, some individuals are sure to be overlooked, and the inevitable alternative presents itself that the ultimate responsibility should be with the community.

Because the case is so strong for community responsibility (whether complementary to private arrangements or not) there is ample justification to retain, in the short run, an illogical scheme that under certain circumstances pays more than the minimum in benefits, so that, when the time is ripe, it may be amended and adjusted to meet the full requirements of those incapacitated from whatever cause.

It is no part of this study to suggest how the details of a national scheme would be worked out. But, that the ultimate aim of making good financial loss to those incapacitated for work, not only from industrial injury but from any cause, should, in the long run, be a national responsibility, would seem a self-evident proposition to any progressive community.

3. *The Blameworthy*

Returning to the more restricted picture of industrial accidents, it is not likely that they are actuated by malice. But apathy, thoughtlessness, meanness in not installing safety devices, and laziness in not promoting safety schemes can sometimes build up to negligence of so aggravated a character that it almost amounts to malice. The law, however, is not primarily concerned with motives, but with action. Where there is a breach of statutory duty, the responsible party may be criminally liable as well as civilly negligent; a complicated situation, the product of centuries of history, and one that is ripe for fundamental review. The policy of recovering loss through another's negligence by invoking the aid of the civil courts might have been suitable to a horse and cart economy, but the requirements of the modern age call for something less chancy, less partial, less expensive to the injured party than this. That it should be used as a means of punishment is contrary to the whole spirit of the times. If a person is blameworthy it is the duty of the community to bring this fact home to him, and to benefit from any levy that is exacted. It is not an individual and civil matter.

Much of the action in the criminal courts may also be thought somewhat out of date. For most of it is initiated and even prosecuted by the factory inspectors, who, whatever their background training, are seldom qualified lawyers. Moreover, the scale of penalties, particularly the financial ones, seems to be geared to the one-man employer rather than the large firm, so often the defendant in modern times. A glance at the number of prosecutions laid (see Part I, p. 43), and the number successful (over 90 per cent) each year leads one to believe that cases are seldom brought unless they are nearly a certainty. Many blameworthy people are apparently not being prosecuted because the case may fail. It is thought in some quarters that the civil courts are dealing with many a case which more properly should have appeared in the criminal courts, and that the justification for maintaining the private recourse to litigation (apart from the need to recover loss), is the reluctance to invoke criminal action. If this is so, it is clearly time further light were thrown on the matter, so that offenders could be dealt with in the right place and in a constructive way.

If there is any relevance in the foregoing, it would seem there is a strong case for establishing a government committee of inquiry, not so much to deal with the safety issue, since in the long run this is too diverse a matter to be confined to the terms of reference of a committee, but to do some re-thinking on the second and third issues mentioned above. It is not enough to examine the industrial injuries scheme and propose amendments, or to consider the alternative remedies as a separate matter. They should be thought of together, so that people who cannot work through sickness or injury may be so paid, or insured or compensated that they do not have to suffer financial loss as well as health loss. The question of negligence is quite separate and should not be tied to financial compensation to the injured, or to the initiative of the injured, but should be the responsibility and prerogative of the state itself.

SELECTED BIBLIOGRAPHY

British Medical Association, *First Aid in Industry*, B.M.A., 1939.

British Medical Association, *The Future of Occupational Health Services*, B.M.A., 1961.

Burnet, J., *Outline of Industrial Medicine, Legislation and Hygiene*, John Wright & Sons Ltd., 1953.

Dinsdale, W. A., *History of Accident Insurance in Great Britain*, Stone & Cox Ltd., 1954, Buckley Press Ltd., 1956.

Gray, H. R., *The Law of Civil Injuries*, Hutchinson, 1955.

Hall, M. P., *Social Services of Modern England*, Routledge, 1958.

Heinrich, H. W. & Granniss, E. R., *Industrial Accident Prevention*, McGraw-Hill, 1959.

Hunter, D., *Health in Industry*, Penguin Books Ltd., 1959.

International Labour Office, *Methods of Statistics of Industrial Injuries*, Geneva, I.L.O., 1947.

International Labour Office, *Accident Prevention – A Worker's Manual*, Geneva, I.L.O., 1961.

King, G. S., *The Ministry of Pensions & National Insurance*, Allen & Unwin, 1958.

Lawson, F. H., *Negligence in the Civil Law*, Clarendon Press, 1950.

Lloyd-Davies, T. A., *The Practice of Industrial Medicine*, J. & A. Churchill Ltd., 1948.

Macleod, I. & Powell, J. E., *The Social Services, Needs and Means*, Conservative Political Centre, 1952.

Munkman, J., *Employers' Liability at Common Law*, Butterworth, 1959.

Parsons, O. H., *Accidents at Work*, Labour Research Dept., 1948.

Passmore, R. & Swanston, C. N., *Industrial Health*, E. & S. Livingstone Ltd., 1950.

Potter, D. & Stansfield, D. H., *National Insurance (Industrial Injuries)*, Butterworth, 1950.

Rowntree, H., *Common Law Liability*, Buckley Press Ltd., 1951.

Street, H., *Principles of the Law of Damages*, Sweet & Maxwell, 1962.

Taylor (Lord), *First Aid in the Factory*, Longmans, 1960.

VESTER, H. & CARTWRIGHT, H. A., *Industrial Injuries* (2 vols.), Sweet & Maxwell, 1961.
WILLIAMS, J. L., *Accidents and Ill-Health at Work*, Staples Press, 1960.
WILSON, A. & LEVY, H., *Workmen's Compensation* (2 vols.), Oxford University Press, 1939.
UNITED NATIONS, *Rehabilitation of the Handicapped*, New York, U.N., 1953.

Government Publications

1920 Cmd. 816, xxvi, *Workmen's Compensation*. Departmental Committee (Holman Gregory, Ch.). Report.
1926 Non-Parl. Medical Research Council, *A Contribution to the Study of the Human Factor in the Causation of Accidents*. By E. M. Newbold. (Industrial Fatigue Research Board Report No. 34.)
1932, 1933, 1936 Non-Parl. Home Office, *Compensation for Industrial Diseases*. Departmental Committee. 1st, 2nd and 3rd Reports.
1937, 1939 Non-Parl. Home Office, Min. of Health, Scottish Office, *Rehabilitation of Persons Injured by Accidents*. Inter-Departmental Committee (Delevingne, Ch.), Interim and Final Reports.
1936–7 Cmd. 5528, xii, *Compulsory Insurance*. Committee (Cassel, Ch.). Report.
1937–8 Cmd. 5657, xv, *Certain Questions Arising Under the Workmen's Compensation Acts*. Departmental Committee (Stewart, Ch.). Report.
1942–3 Cmd. 6404, vi, *Social Insurance and Allied Services*. Inter-Departmental Committee (Beveridge, Ch.). Report.
1942–3 Cmd. 6415, vi, *Rehabilitation and Resettlement of Disabled Persons*. Inter-Departmental Committee (Tomlinson, Ch.). Report.
1943–4 Cmd. 6551, viii, *Social Insurance. Part II. Workmen's Compensation*
7 & 8 Geo. 6. c. 10, *Disabled Persons (Employment) Act, 1944*.
1944–5 Cmd. 6580, Cmd. 6642, vi, 1945–6 Cmd. 6860, xiii, *Workmen's Compensation. Alternative Remedies*. Departmental Committee (Monckton, Ch.). Interim. 2nd Interim and Final Reports.
1946, 1949 Non-Parl. Min. of Labour, *Rehabilitation and Resettlement of Disabled Persons*. Standing Committee. Reports.
9 & 10 Geo. 6. c. 62, *National Insurance (Industrial Injuries) Act, 1946*.
1950–1 Cmd. 8170, xv, *Industrial Health Services*. Committee (Dale, Ch.). Report.
1952–3 Cmd. 8963, xi, *Employment of Older Men and Women*. National Advisory Committee. 1st Report.
1954–5 (22) vi, 1959–60 (300) xvii, *National Insurance (Industrial Injuries) Act, 1946*. Reports by Government Actuary on 1st and 2nd Quinquennial Reviews.

1955–6 Cmd. 9883, xiv, *Rehabilitation, Training and Resettlement of Disabled Persons*. Committee (Piercy, Ch.). Report.
1956 Non-Parl. Min. of Labour, *Industrial Accident Prevention*. National Joint Advisory Council, Industrial Safety Sub-Committee. Report.
1956–7 Cmnd. 218, viii, *Administrative Tribunals and Enquiries*. Committee (Franks, Ch.). Report.
1958–9 Cmnd. 736, xxv. *Duties, Organisation and Staffing of the Medical Branch of the Factory Inspectorate*.
1960 Non-Parl. Min. of Labour. *Guide to Statistics Collected by H.M. Factory Inspectorate*.
1959–60 Cmnd. 953, ix, *Safety and Health in the Building and Civil Engineering Industries, 1954–8*. Report.
1961 Non-Parl. Min. of Pensions & National Insurance, *Law Relating to National Insurance (Industrial Injuries)*, and Supplements to 1962.
1961 Non-Parl. Min. of Power, *Digest of Pneumoconiosis Statistics*, 1960.
1962 Non-Parl. Min. of Health. *Accident and Emergency Services*. Central Health Services Council. Standing Medical Advisory Committee. Sub-Committee (Platt, Ch.). Report.
Annual Reports of the Ministry of National Insurance (from 1953, the Ministry of Pensions and National Insurance) 1949–62.
Annual Reports of the Chief Inspector of Factories 1949–62.

INDEX

Index

Index

For Product Safety Concerns and Information please contact our EU
representative GPSR@taylorandfrancis.com
Taylor & Francis Verlag GmbH, Kaufingerstraße 24, 80331 München, Germany

www.ingramcontent.com/pod-product-compliance
Ingram Content Group UK Ltd.
Pitfield, Milton Keynes, MK11 3LW, UK
UKHW022156190926
475702UK00003B/61
* 9 7 8 0 4 1 5 1 7 6 7 7 4 *